# Called to Care
## Ministering to Special Populations in our Communities and Churches

*A COMPASSIONATE CARE RESOURCE FOR THOSE IN THE PEW DESIRING TO HELP*

DR. PATRICIA LOTT

Called to Care:
Ministering to Special Populations within Our Churches
Copyright @ 2015 Shacklebuster Ministries

All Scripture Quotations unless otherwise stated are taken from
the King James Version of the Bible

Requests for workshop / information should be addressed to:
Dr. Patricia Lott
Shacklebuster Ministries
schacklebusterconference@yahoo.com

ISBN: 13: 978-0-9827592-2-6

Printed in the United States of America

~ Dedication ~

This book is lovingly dedicated to my son Elder Michael A. Lott Sr., who has from his earliest years on this earth has been "filled with compassion" to the point that even in his degree choice included and emphasis in "special populations". Come son, let us snatch them as it were from the fire and love them back to life.

~ Author's Note ~

First and foremost I want to thank the Lord for blessing me with three children "Filled with Compassion" I cannot begin to tell you about all of the people that have come through our home because of this. I will never forget my daughter filling her backpack with food, putting it on our dog's back and heading out of the house to "Go feed the children in Somalia" Nor will I forget a closed door conversation with my oldest son on how to help a classmate who he described as "the walking dead because of church hurt" Each of them have book series dedicated to them.

Then there is Stu, one of the most challenging students I have ever had. Once on fire for the Lord something happened to make him doubt and question. However, for one straight year on each break and after each class we had deep heart impacting conversations in which the compassionate Christ resonated. I can never forget nor count how many conversations included the phrase "and I bet he/she couldn't even talk to anyone at church because of how judgmental and uncompassionate the church people are." Those conversations sparked the beginning workings of this book.

Last but in no way least I want to thank my Lord and Savior Jesus Christ for being the ultimate model of compassion. I thank Him for challenging me one day in 2008 during revival in Vallejo, CA as I was preparing to speak with one simple question, *"Patti, Do you **really** want to be like Me?"* Never in my wildest dreams did I understand that my simple yes that day in that hotel room was going to set my feet on the path that it has. There have been many transformational experiences that have changed me from the "little Philly girl who is trying to get back home (heaven) to her father (not biological)" into one who in every way, everyday endeavors to be like Jesus. I have noticed things previously missed, I have acted on things previously ignored,

I have walked in places I never dreamed of taking myself and one day not 2 years ago I stopped and saw the bush that burned and was not consumed. The result of that experience was a heart filled and a life moved with compassion. In the words of the Apostle John, "And there are also many other things which Jesus did, the which, if they should be written every one, I suppose that even the world itself could not contain the books that should be written. Amen."

# TABLE OF CONTENT

*"Love and compassion are necessities, not luxuries. Without them humanity cannot survive."— Dalai Lama*

# ACKNOWLEDGMENTS

I would like to take the time to thank my Sister of the Soul Gwendolyn E. Lawson-Townsend, my oldest son Wayne S. Lott and my husband Pastor Wayne Lott Sr. for all of the time that they spent reading and correcting and helping me bring these pages to life. You are wonderful and I look forward to seeing you at a Called to Care Workshop real soon.

# ~INTRODUCTION~

When one hears the phrase "Compassionate Care" one often has visions of a hospice situation in which a person is transitioning from life as we recognize it to what we call death. The goal is to make this transition as painless as possible. Something else is seen in this situation and that is a person surrounded by people who love and care about them.

In this book we will explore another type of compassionate care. What I want to look at is the way we can care compassionately to those whom the Lord brings into our awareness each and every day. The word Compassion is listed in the Bible 40 times. Six times we read that Jesus "was *moved* with compassion" or "*had* compassion on someone" 1 John 3:17 poses us a very piercing question. One that should cause each of us to have a serious conversation with ourselves concerning our living of the scriptures in our congregations and communities. It is the foundation and purpose of this book. This one verse reads "But whoso hath this world's good, and seeth his brother hath need, and shutteth up his bowels of compassion, how dwelleth the love of God in him?"

Just think about it. This verse says nothing about having an abundance of finances. It is speaking to having a heart like Jesus who is moved to do something based on what one see's in another's situation. I am not talking about donating money to organizations and social services. I am talking about making a difference in your corner of the world, in your bubble of existence, in your congregation and in your community.

However, in order to do that we have to open our eyes and our *hearts* to what is right in front of us. If we will look at the historical event of Moses' call to be the deliverer of Egypt it looks something like this. Moses is out in the field tending to the flocks of Jethro his father in law. Moses stopped and looked at a bush. What he saw was a bush that burned but was not consumed with fire. In looking he could recognize the angel of the Lord appearing to him out of the bush. He was able to hear what the Lord was trying to tell him and be launched into his kingdom assignment (Ex 3:1-4) I bring this up on the starting line of our journey for the following reasons: 1) There are people who we sit next to or in close proximity to in our congregations service after service who are literally drowning in the experience of their season. They are hurting, they are confused, and they are in need. Not a material need, not a soul need, but a compassionate need. They need someone to "See" that they are burning but thanks be to God, they have not been consumed. There are people in our communities whom we pass every day. They are not going to disappear. They are not nuisances. They are opportunities for ministry. No they are not prime candidates for you to recruit them to your church. They are not prospective tithers. They may never even be able to repay you for what you do. Who they are, believe it or not, are the very ones that our Savior stopped to spend time with, listen to, and to *see* simply because they needed it. Jesus was not recruiting followers when he encountered the woman caught in the act of adultery, the Centurion soldier whose daughter had died, or the man whose son was what we would label today as special needs. "And seeing them he was moved with compassion," meaning that he could not just look on them and do nothing about it. He was moved to action. That is what he is asking of us. To actually see and then act.

The first thing that I am asking you to do is to stir up the compassion that our Savior placed inside of you. If He lives in you then you have compassion coursing through your heart. Let's do a quick examination to check out where we are as we read through the following scenarios. Answer honestly, not as you feel that you should answer. No one is reading this book except for you.

- ***Do I have the ability to meet people where they are while remembering that I am simply God's grace away from being in that same situation?*** For example, you may not have had a family member incarcerated or deployed. However, you can remember what it was like to have your family separated without the ability to prevent the societal biases that accompany that separation. You can also remember what it was like to feel helpless to change a situation while trying your best to live with your head held high and your hope in Jesus Christ. It is here that you will be able to begin the foundation of compassionately caring for those around you.
- ***Do I have the ability to allow myself to feel (not analyze or intellectualize) what a person or family is feeling?*** For example, you may have never been molested so you do not know firsthand what that feels like. However, we have all had situations in which our trust was betrayed, we were violated in some way and our sense of security has been shaken. These are the same feelings that this precious child of God has experienced. So while molestation is not our experience the feelings that accompany them are. It is at this place that we can join with compassion and help begin the healing process that will redirect them back to Christ.
- You may have never questioned your sexuality, ***but can you remember a time in which you questioned the plan God had for you or questioned which direction you should take?*** Have you felt the pressure to conform

to societal norms that seemed foreign to you? Have you made a stand for Christ that others didn't understand so they unintentionally distanced themselves from you and you felt left alone to try and figure things out while there was a war raging inside of you? These memories will help you to interact in a more compassionate way with those brought into your path.

We must begin here. Reentering into these emotions take a lot of energy out of us and brings up many memories that we would rather forget. Yet, it is in this place that compassion is born.

If we must hear another's emotional pain and another's struggles during their current season, then we must without a doubt be prepared to hear between the words, see beyond our senses and carry a load that is not our own. Everyone has a story behind their struggle and it is the story that needs to be shared, heard and understood even if not condoned. We must remember that it was while we were YET sinners that Christ died for us...for them. (Romans 5:8)

One last thing I would like to touch on before we begin this journey together and that is the need for a mind change, vocabulary change and a paradigm shift inside of you. Sometime the words and phrases that we use in passing have lost their meaning and power. Sometimes the words and phrases that we use do way more damage than we even imagined simply because they are just things that we have acclimated into our way of communicating. They have no understanding, they have no depth. The scripture says "Death and life are in the power of the tongue: and they that love it shall eat the fruit thereof" Proverbs 18:21. It is the Spirit that quickeneth; the flesh profiteth nothing: the words that I speak unto you, they are spirit and they are life" John 6:63" These special population persons are teetering on death. They are doing the best that they can with what they have been asked to endure. Your words literally have the power to bring hope and healing or discouragement and despair. Have you ever said to a loved one, "I just love you to death?" Have you ever thought about what you were actually saying? How many batterers loved their wife to death? How many pedophiles loved that child to death? How many "church hurt" people have been loved to death in the congregation? Throughout this book you will see a new phrase, "I Love you to LIFE!" That is what we are going to be learning to do as we travel throughout this book. Learning to Love one another to LIFE!

What a journey it is that lies ahead of us as we explore the world of these special populations to which we wish to minister compassion to in our congregations and communities. During our time together in this book we will be faced with information that causes us to look deep within ourselves and give out of ourselves on very intimate and holy levels. This level of compassion takes skill as well as energy and it is wonderful to know that the Holy Spirit has equipped each and every one of us with what we need to be successful. So as you begin your journey remember not to fear…just love maturely because perfect love casteth out fear (1 John 4:18).

Let us begin our journey with a word of Prayer:

God, I turn my will and my life over to You this day for Your keeping. Your will, Lord, not mine. I ask for Your guidance and direction. I will walk humbly with You and my fellow man.
You are giving me a grateful heart for my many blessings. You are removing the defects of character that stand in my way. You are giving me freedom from self-will.

Let love, compassion, and understanding be in every thought, word, and deed this day. I truly desire Your abundance of truth, love, harmony and peace. As I go out today to do Your bidding,
let me help anyone I can who is less fortunate than I.

Amen

DR. PATRICIA LOTT

# ~ *Before Care* ~

*Prepare thy work without, and make it fit for thyself in the field; and afterwards build thine house.  Pr 24:27*

It is a given that today's individual has a work week that our parents and grandparents would shake their heads at. We strive to accomplish so much. Many families are forced to be 2 income earning families simply to keep a modest roof and minimal food a reality. However the 2015 individual is also very egocentric. The focus is more on me and my three to use a phrase I grew up with. Our parents and grandparents took little and made much. Today we have much and it amounts to very little. The difference is that our parents and grandparents would make provision for those less fortunate. There was always something out of their need for someone else. The most important thing is that they found time to rest, to do self-care, to prepare mentally and physically for what each new day would bring. Many times we the body of Christ, fill so much into our Saturdays that we awaken tired on Sunday morning. In addition many of us are in such a rushed state to make it to church on time that we arrive a little discombobulated. We simply want to fall into the Lord's presence and allow him to make all things new…for us. Can you identify with this? Many times it is when we are in this state that the Lord designs what I like to call a "Mission Encounter for us" Revisiting the book of Exodus third chapter, Moses states, "I will now turn aside, and see this great sight, why the bush is not burnt." I had the experience of being in that part of the world. It is a common occurrence that bushes spontaneously combust and as quickly as they catch on fire, the fire goes out. No doubt Moses had seen burning bushes a lot during his time tending the flocks. He was busy, he was preoccupied, he was working and he was tired. However, this particular day the burning of a bush caught his attention and he had to attend to it. In so doing his life was forever changed and the works of God were made manifest in him through the saving of a nation. So it will be with those that you are about to minister compassionately to. No doubt they have been in the church for some time. No doubt they have been dealing with these situations for a long time. No doubt many people including you have walked pass them before for various reasons; maybe you just didn't know what to say, perhaps you had a task or assignment that needed your attention, but today, that day, this day you have to stop and take pause and you know that you have to interact with this person, you have to see why the bush is not burnt so to speak. In so doing your life, their life will be forever changed and the works of God will be made manifest in you through the saving, comforting or restoration of a soul.

This need requires us to be in the right place in body, soul and spirit. Here are a few things that we can do to make sure that when God designs the encounter we are up for the task.

(1) **Make sure that you get enough sleep the night before.** Many times when we are tired physically we are short tempered, we are a little more abrasive than normal. We

are rushing to get away so that we can rest and we don't have the energy to give what is needed to see, hear and feel what is in front of us on a deeper level than the surface.

(2) **We need to prepare as much for Sunday as we can on Saturday**. Have the car gassed and packed, have your purse changed ladies, make sure that you have stockings, make sure that you don't have too much to do in the kitchen, have your clothes ironed and your family taken care of as well.

(3) A lot of us like to fast on Sundays, however, you need to make sure that you have some protein in your system and that you are not physically tired. Fasting is to prepare you for the experience. That should be handled prior to entering into the fire, not on the day of the fire.

(4) **Try to wake up early, on purpose, with a purpose**, to be sensitive to the direction of the Lord in leading you to a purposeful encounter with your brother and or sister in need of compassionate care. The snooze button is your enemy when you are trying to be intentional in your compassion.

(5) **Pray, Pray, Pray**. This is not the type of prayer that we do out of routine. This is not the prayer for souls to be saved for the pastor and the needs of the church. This is the type of prayer that transforms _you_. This is the type of praying that opens you up so that you can hear and feel. This is the type of prayer that directs and teaches. This is specific prayer that alerts the Lord that you are ready to be used in this area and that you are willing to let him prepare you for that moment in which he beckons you and entrusts these precious people unto you.

(6) **Study, Study, Study.** This is not the type of studying that you do for Sunday School and Bible Band. This is not the type of studying that you do for your own personal reasons. This is the studying that goes into compassion. This is a search of the scriptures that the Holy Ghost can bring back to your memory dealing with each and every area that we will cover. The Father is waiting on you, The Son is fueling you and the Spirit is uploading into you. Don't try to force the common scriptures. The Lord may want to take you and a scripture that others would think is off to touch the heart of the people. **_All_** scripture is given by inspiration and **_all_** scripture is profitable. Let me give you quick example by way of testimony of what I mean. Three years ago I was diagnosed with cancer in 2 places. I asked the Lord for a word of comfort. Now you may be thinking "He sent His word and healed them," or "I am the Lord that healeth thee" or any number of "healing scriptures" yet the scripture that the Spirit spoke to me is ,"The Egyptian that you see today you will see again nor more forever." Three years later as of this writing people still give me a puzzled look when I share that, yet it is the scripture that kept me going through the times that lay ahead. The point is this. Don't dictate the scripture that you will put in your

compassionate tool box but let the Spirit infuse you. During our journey together in this book I will offer you some scriptures, however, it is easier to use the scriptures that the Lord gives to you as they will be tailor given to you for your use with those whom He brings to you. Let's begin creating our "Bag of Scriptures" now. As the Lord gives them to you, write them down, commit them to memory and then let the Lord call them up when necessary.

(7) **Practice patience and pace.** You don't have to hear the entire story at one time. Know your limits and understand that the person whom you are ministering to has limits as well. Remember that a baby step is still a step. God didn't create the world in 1 day and the people that we are trying to help can't be helped in one conversation. This time of preparation is where you can learn your limitations, learn how well you actually hear, gain comfort with the use of your scriptures. You want to leave this time of preparation as a skillful warrior.

As you can see, it is important that we properly prepare to be effective in our ministering to those who come into our path. In the world something that we use something called "the 7 P's" Poor Prior Planning Produces Poor Performance Proficiency. If we manage to remember this in our everyday living and functioning, how much more should we be mindful of them when we seek to impact the kingdom for our Lord?

~ Prayer ~

Father I come to you today thanking you for awakening me to the needs that are around me. For those who sit in worship with me, empower me at the appropriate time to demonstrate the care compassionately that they need. For those in my community, the teacher, the technician, the plumber, the construction worker, the homeless, helpless and infirmed that I see every day, it is my prayer that you find me ready and worthy to schedule a mission encounter that I may manifest your love to them.

-Amen

# ~ *GRIEF AND LOSS* ~

*"Thus saith the LORD; A voice was heard in Ramah, lamentation, and bitter weeping; Rachel weeping for her children refused to be comforted for her children, because they were not." Jeremiah 31:15*

Grieving is something that all of us are familiar with. We grieve over the loss of many things: our youth, a relationship, a job, the way society used to be and much, much more. At times it appears that grieving is something that we have become desensitized to. With the initial hearing of the death we are there, cakes and meals in hand, helping with arrangements and appearing at the ceremony being ever so conscientious to have our paper signed to take to our employer to ensure payment for the time that we were away from the office to mourn the death. Employers decide who we are to grieve over the most and whom they will grant the 3 days bereavement leave for (parent, spouse or child). Two week later we are all expected to be back to our normal schedules full of smiles, and laughter, lest by any means our tears make others uncomfortable. With this in mind let's take a few moments to reacquaint ourselves with: grieving, mourning and loss. (def: Merriam Webster Dictionary)

**Loss**: the experience of having something (someone) taken from you or destroyed; the harm or privation (the state of being deprived) resulting from loss or separation

**Grief**: deep sadness caused especially by someone's death

**Mourn**: to feel and show great sadness because someone has died

Simply put, someone has had a loved one, in terms of this training, a child or spouse taken away from them resulting in the pain of being deprived of that love, companionship and presence. This has caused a deep sadness the likes of which cannot be fully comprehended without experience. Regardless to how much we sympathize with this life changing event, unless we have stood by the graveside of our spouse or our child we can never "know" what our sister or brother is going through. Yet there is a compassion in our very core to help in some way to make it better. That is what we will spend our time together in this chapter talking about. How can I help this population in some small way to navigate through this devastating period of life?

We have found 5 very common reactions to death that Elisabeth Kubeler Ross termed the Five Stages of Greif and Loss. These stages will be reviewed here because simply put, the stage that the person we want to compassionately minister to is in will determine the manner in which we effectively minister to them. The five stages, denial, anger, bargaining, depression and acceptance are a part of the framework that makes up our learning to live without the one we have lost. They are tools to help us frame and identify what we may be feeling. But they are not stops on some linear timeline in grief. Not everyone goes through all of them or in a prescribed order. Our hope is that with these stages comes the knowledge of grief's terrain, making us better equipped to cope with life and loss. They are responses to loss that many people have, but there is not a typical response to loss just as there is no typical loss. Our grief is as individual as our lives.

**Denial**: This first stage of grieving helps us to survive the loss. In this stage, the world becomes meaningless and overwhelming. Life makes no sense. We are in a state of shock and denial. We go numb. We wonder how we can go on, if we can go on, why we should go on. We try to find a way to simply get through each day. Denial and shock help us to cope and make survival possible. Denial helps us to pace our feelings of grief. There is a grace in denial. It is perhaps one of God's ways of letting in only as much as we can handle. As one accepts the reality of their loss and start to ask oneself questions, one is unknowingly beginning the healing process. He/she is becoming stronger, and the denial is beginning to fade. But as they proceed, all the feelings they were denying begin to surface.

**Anger:** Anger is a necessary stage of the healing process. Be willing to allow people to feel their anger, even though it may seem endless. The more it is truly felt, the more it will begin to dissipate and the more they will heal. There are many other emotions under that anger and they will get to them in time, but anger is the emotion we are most used to managing. The truth is that anger has no limits. It can extend not only to their friends, the doctors, their family, him or herself and the loved one who died and to YOU, but also to God. Regardless to their faith they may ask, "Where is God in this? Underneath anger is pain, (remember our definitions?). It is natural to feel deserted and abandoned, but we live in a society that fears anger. Yes, even in the church. However, anger is strength and it can be an anchor, giving temporary structure to the nothingness of loss. At first grief feels like being lost at sea: no connection to anything. Then the one left behind gets angry at someone, maybe it is a person who didn't attend the funeral, maybe a person who isn't around, maybe a person who is different now that their loved one has died. Suddenly he/she has a structure – – their anger toward them. The anger becomes a bridge over the open sea, a connection from them to that person. It is something to hold onto; and a connection made from the strength of anger feels better than nothing. We usually know more about suppressing anger than feeling it. The anger is just another indication of the intensity of that person's love. There is an old Star Trek episode that comes to mind when an alien wanted to take Captain Kirk's pain away. Kirk replied. "I want my pain I need my pain." This is the story with grief's anger. It is necessary. It is not pleasant but neither is castor oil, like castor oil anger serves a necessary purpose. Your job is to not take it personally, not try and get them to move away from it prematurely, but to be a safe place

**Bargaining:** Before a loss, it seems like a person will do anything if only their loved one would be spared. "Please God," they bargain, "I will never be angry at my spouse/ child / parent again if you'll just let him/her live." After a loss, bargaining may take the form of a temporary truce. "What if I devote the rest of my life to helping others? Then can I wake up and realize this has all been a bad dream?" We become lost in a maze of "If only…" or "What if…" statements. We want life returned to what is was; we want our loved one restored. We want to go back in time: find the tumor sooner, recognize the illness more quickly, stop the accident from happening…if only, if only, if only. Guilt is often bargaining's companion. The "if onlys" cause us to find fault in ourselves and what we "think" we could have done differently. We may even bargain with the pain. We will do anything not to feel the pain of this loss. We remain in the past, trying to negotiate our way out of the hurt. People often think of the stages as lasting weeks or months. They forget that the stages are responses to feelings that can last for minutes or hours as we flip in and out of one and then another. We do not enter and leave each individual stage in a linear fashion. We may feel one, then another and back again to the first one.

**Depression:** After bargaining, our attention moves squarely into the present. Empty feelings present themselves, and grief enters our lives on a deeper level, deeper than we ever imagined. This depressive stage feels as though it will last forever. It's important to understand that this depression is *not* a sign of mental illness. It is the appropriate response to a great loss. We withdraw from life, left in a fog of intense sadness, wondering, perhaps, if there is any point in going on alone. Why go on at all? Depression after a loss is too often seen as unnatural: a state to be fixed, something to snap out of. The first question to ask yourself is whether or not the situation that this person is in is actually depressing. The loss of a spouse or a child is a very depressing situation, and depression is a normal and appropriate response. To not experience depression after a loved one dies would be unusual. When a loss fully settles in your soul, the realization that your loved one didn't get better this time and is not coming back is understandably depressing. If grief is a process of healing, then depression is one of the many necessary steps along the way. * Mental Health Professionals will not even diagnose someone with Depression or an Adjustment Disorder who has experienced the loss of a loved one until after 2 years. Give this person a break. Pay attention to their diet. Prepare food for them that are rich in dopamine, serotonin and norepinephrine. These will help to naturally help fight the depression that you see. Many times the one who is grieving is not eating or eating properly. This sets them up for a deficiency in these neurotransmitters. Isn't it wonderful the way that the Lord weaved us together? Don't send them to counseling, help them to eat to combat the bodily deficiency that has happened as a result of their intense grieving. These foods are:

## SERETONIN
### Tryptophan

| Turkey | Tuna | Soybeans | Beef | Lamb | Halibut |
| Shrimp | Salmon Seeds | Bananas | Dairy Products | | Nuts |

## DOPAMINE
### Tryosine

| Apples | Beets | Celery | Chicken |
| Cucumbers | Honey | Tofu | Sweet Peppers |
| Watermelon | Beans Leafy Green Veggies | | |

## NORAEPINEPHRINE (noradrenalin / EPINEPHERINE (adrenaline)

| Chicken | Fish | Nuts |

**Acceptance:** Acceptance is often confused with the notion of being "all right" or "OK" with what has happened. This is not the case. Most people don't ever feel OK or all right about the loss of a spouse or child. This stage is about accepting the reality that our loved one is physically gone and recognizing that this new reality is the permanent reality. We will never like this reality or make it OK, but eventually we accept it. We learn to live with it. It is the new norm with which we must learn to live. We must try to live now in a world where our loved one is missing. In resisting this new norm, at first many people want to maintain life as it was before a loved one died. In time, through bits and pieces of acceptance, however, we see that we cannot maintain the past intact. It has been forever changed and we must readjust. We must learn to reorganize roles, reassign them to others or take them on ourselves. Finding acceptance may be just having more good days than bad ones. As we begin to live again and enjoy life, we often feel that in doing so, we are betraying our loved one. We can never replace what has been lost, but we can make new connections, new meaningful relationships, new inter-dependencies. Instead of denying feelings, we listen to our needs; we move, we change, we grow, we evolve. We may start to reach out to others and become involved in their lives. We invest in our friendships and in our relationship with ourselves. We begin to live again, but we cannot do so until we have given grief its time.

Now that we understand what grief, loss, mourning and the stages that one goes through while grieving the question becomes: What makes the death of a spouse and a child so special that we must move them to separate categories. To understand this let's turn to the ultimate authority…the Holy Scriptures:

## THE GREIVING SPOUSE

Genesis 2:18-25 "*18 And the LORD God said, It is not good that the man should be alone; I will make him an help meet for him. 19 And out of the ground the LORD God formed every beast of the field, and every fowl of the air; and brought them unto Adam to see what he would call them: and whatsoever Adam called every living creature that was the name thereof. 20 And Adam gave names to all cattle, and to the fowl of the air, and to every beast of the field; but for Adam there was not found an help meet for him. 21 And the LORD God caused a deep sleep to fall upon Adam, and he slept : and he took one of his ribs, and closed up the flesh instead thereof; 22 And the rib, which the LORD God had taken from man, made he a woman, and brought her unto the man. 23 And Adam said , This is now bone of my bones, and flesh of my flesh: she shall be called Woman, because she was taken out of Man. 24 Therefore shall a man leave his father and his mother, and shall cleave unto his wife: and they shall be one flesh. 25 And they were both naked, the man and his wife, and were not ashamed.*"

There is something very unique and spiritual about marriage. The book of beginnings states that it was God Himself who stated that man should not be alone. His remedy was to "Create" woman for the man. This creation was very specific and purposeful. He took woman out of man. That rib was a connecting factor for the man had to lose it in order for the woman to be fashioned for him. The woman was presented to the man and as verse 24 states, they became one flesh. They became one in purpose. They became one in vision. They became one in goals, values, direction and mission. They became inseparable. Verse 25 goes on to say that they were both naked, the man and his wife and were not ashamed. They knew one another's strengths & weaknesses. They knew one another's goals and desires, their appetites and drives. There was nothing secret or hidden and they were free to be so with one another. Why? Because they are one, just opposite sides of the same coin. When a woman or man has loss a spouse, someone with whom they have lived with for more years than their parents is taken away from them. When someone loses their spouse a very real and very intimate portion of themselves has been wrenched away, cut out from them. The soft touch the strong shoulder, the magic of ordinary days ceases to exist.

Coming home to an empty house is not easy for this person in your congregation or community. There is no one to greet them, and the chair opposite theirs at the dinner table is empty. The house seems to echo from the silence and they shed tears as they remember that they are now alone. So many years together, so many memories that the two of them created together are all that he/ she has left. Losing a spouse has changed their entire life, especially when the loved one was also that person's best friend. They feel completely lost and totally uncomfortable making even minor decisions. The bed feels big and many of them are hugging the pillows for comfort. There is something inside of them that tells them that they *can* and must survive! Yet they can't seem to grab a hold of it. This hurts way too much. This my reader, is where you come in. It is your ability to be compassionate to this situation that can snatch this person back as it were from the fire.

When someone we care about or dearly love loses a husband, a wife, or a partner, it is a shock to everyone around them. It can be almost impossible to know how to help someone who has lost this love of their life. Here are some tips for helping your loved one work through their grief over the loss of their partner.

## *WHAT IS NEEDED*

**What to Do**

- It's common to misunderstand how long it takes a bereaved individual to adjust to a new life. Some may adjust more easily than others. Stay close to this person as their life changes - it's a long battle.
- Be present - they have just suffered a major loss.
- Listen non-judgmentally and compassionately. Your kindness will never be forgotten.
- Remind yourself that grief is as unique as the person experiencing it - there's no right or wrong way to grieve. Grief simply *is*.
- Help this person to organize any paperwork, medical bills, and other things associated with spouse loss. That way, bills are paid on time, and this person doesn't feel he or she has one more thing to deal with.
- Reach out to this person. Call. Keep calling. Send text messages. Email. Do this frequently, even if they do not respond. Sometimes it's all they can do to survive. But know that hearing from you can make a world of difference.
- Continue reaching out, long after the funeral has ended. Support, by then, has probably dropped off, and it's likely that this person is really beginning to feel the loss of his or her partner.
- Remember anniversary dates and help this person during these awful times. Birthdays, anniversaries, the day of the loved one's death - these are all days that will be a lot harder from now on. Help by remembering to call, send a card, visit, or otherwise be there for them.
- Cook frozen meals that can be easily heated up. Many grieving people forget to eat, so having something around that's easily prepare-able can make a huge difference...especially during the first few months after the death.
- Offer practical help - do a load of laundry while you're visiting. Pick up some groceries at the store. Offer to run errands or accompany this person on errands. Grief makes it very hard to do even the simplest things - sometimes having someone else around can give them the strength to brave the store or pharmacy.
- Losing a spouse, especially if they've been married for many years, will make them feel more alone than they ever have. If possible, spend some time just being with them. It's hard going from being a twosome to a single.
- Offer to go to weddings, funerals, and other situations in which their spouse's absence won't feel as devastating.
- Have a weekly dinner arranged to go out (or stay in) with them to give them something to look forward to.

- So many of us want to "fix" the situation for others, but it's impossible. We cannot fix people, we cannot replace their spouse - what we can be is a friend. Be there to love them and support them.
- Be patient with this person. The range of emotions that grief puts us through runs from depression and anger to guilt and sadness. Patience is necessary and important.
- Let them talk about all of the ugly emotions they might be feeling - allow them to do so in such a way that they do not feel as though you are judging them.
- There may be legal issues involved if the deceased has a complicated family situation (overbearing in-laws, stepchildren, ex-spouse). Offer to help navigate the waters of how to grieve while dealing with the emotions of others closely involved.
- Your Sister in the Lord, especially if you still have a partner, may not want to discuss their loss with you. It's almost impossible to know the unique pain of losing a partner unless you have been there yourself. If the one grieving does not feel comfortable discussing the loss of their spouse, suggest local support groups for bereaved individuals.
- Remember: you don't have to have been a close friend to support. It's appreciated that you care.
- Remember that the pain of losing a partner will never heal.

## What NOT to Do

- Do not expect that this person will "get over" their loss on a set time-table. Grief and grieving is unique to each person.
- Don't change the subject if the deceased individual comes up in conversation. It may be uncomfortable for you to talk about, but the person who is grieving wants to feel as though their husband or wife is not forgotten.
- Don't use "he" or "she" in conversation while referring to the deceased. Use their *name*.
- As everyone grieves in their own way, don't chastise someone for being "too happy too soon" or "wallowing."
- Should this person begin to date "too soon" after the loss of their spouse, remember that it's neither your place to judge or understand coping mechanisms. Pray for and with them.
- As always, avoid platitudes. Special mention goes to "He or she is in a better place." It's dismissive of the tremendous loss, and without knowing the religious background of your grief-stricken person you are attempting to help, it may not be something they actually believe.

DR. PATRICIA LOTT

- Don't say, "I know just how you feel." Unless you, too, have lost a spouse, you do not know how they feel. That comment can cause a lot of anger as it feels dismissive of the loss.
- Don't make assumptions about the grieving person based upon how they appear. Some people are excellent at hiding their emotions.
- Do not dismiss this person's varying range of emotions. Because we each grieve in our own way, we may not experience the same emotions - there are no right or wrong emotions involved in the grieving process.
- Avoid telling this person about your own grief experiences.
- Do not compare grief - grief is different for everyone.
- Do not offer unsolicited advice about "getting over" their grief. They will NEVER be over their grief.
- Don't offer reasoning about how they should or shouldn't feel.

It's hard to know what to say to someone who has lost a spouse. Let's talk a little bit about what TO say to someone who has lost their husband or wife, as well as what NOT to say.

## WHAT CAN YOU SAY

- Acknowledge the death by saying, "I just heard that your husband (or wife) died. I am here if you want to talk about him (or her)."
- Express concern, "I'm so very sorry that you lost your wife (or husband)."
- Be genuine without hiding your feelings, "I wish I knew what to say, but please know how much I care."
- Offer support, "Please tell me what I can do for you."
- Ask questions, "How are you feeling?" without assuming you know how the grieving person feels.

## WHAT YOU SHOULD NOT SAY

- "You'll get remarried someday."
- "He/She was lucky to have lived to such an old age."
- "It was God's will."
- "He's/She's in Heaven now."

- "Be thankful he/she is not in pain anymore."
- "Think of all the good times you had."
- "You'll feel better soon."
- "Count your blessings."
- "You have so much to be grateful for."
- "Time heals all wounds."
- "Pull yourself together - be strong!"
- "I know exactly how you feel."

## THE GREIVING PARENT

Jeremiah 31:15 "Thus saith the LORD; A voice was heard in Ramah, lamentation, and bitter weeping; Rahel weeping for her children refused to be comforted for her children, because they were not."

This scripture depicts the indescribable pain that accompanies the death of a child. Just imagine Rahel who just a few years ago was welcoming this child into the world, watched this child grow and become, wiped tears, kissed boo-boos, hugged when they were afraid…watched go to the prom, smiled through tears as she watched launch out on their own to college or their own home to begin their life as an adult…whichever stage they are in at the time…hearing the news that her precious baby is dead…living in a world that just not too long ago was filled with the laughter and loving of this child.

The loss of a child is one of the most traumatic and stressful events that a parent will ever endure. The pain and suffering that accompanies this loss is beyond words. Whether it is an anticipatory death from an illness, or the sudden death of an accident this is the worse loss of all. It goes beyond the natural order of things. As much as we love and miss our spouses we know that one of us must leave the other behind…but…we are not supposed to bury our children…and yet, here we are. Because the more natural order is for parents to precede their children in death, this person must readapt to a new and seemingly illogical reality. This shocking reality says that even though you are older and have been the protector and provider, you have survived while your child has not. This many times can be so difficult to comprehend.

Not only has the death of this child violated nature's way, where the young grow up and replace the old, but this person's personal identity was tied to their child. They may feel impotent and wonder why they couldn't have protected their child from death.

The death of a child can result in a variety of emotions. Confusion, disorganization, fear, guilt, anger and relief are just a few of the emotions parents may feel. Sometimes these emotions will follow each other within a short period of time. Or they may occur simultaneously.

As strange as some of these emotions may seem, they are normal and healthy. Allow this person you are trying to minister to the opportunity to learn from these feelings. Don't be surprised if out of nowhere they suddenly experience surges of grief, even at the most unexpected times. These grief attacks can be frightening and leave them feeling overwhelmed. They are, however, a natural response to the death of a child. It's hard to imagine that the world hasn't stopped. It's hard to believe that everything keeps on going. When the horror of losing a child becomes a reality to someone that the Lord has brought into your path, you want to do something - anything - to help someone who has lost a baby, infant, or child. But... *how?* This dear reader, is where you come in.

With the death of a child, whatever the age, one's hopes, dreams and plans for the future are turned upside down. This person is beginning a journey that is often frightening, painful and overwhelming. The death of a child results in the most profound bereavement. In fact, sometimes the feelings of grief may be so intense that this person cannot understand what is happening. So how can you help someone so caught up in this life changing event move toward healing in their personal grief experience?

## *WHAT IS NEEDED*

### What to Do

- When faced with the loss of a child, many people are afraid to say the wrong thing, so they say nothing. This is a mistake. Many people are afraid to bring up the deceased child, fearing it will open wounds and raw feelings. You may think that bringing it up will not help, but this person has not forgotten for one second that her child has passed away - not saying the child's name will only hurt because it will make the grieving parent feel their child is forgotten.

- Send a photo or keepsake with the child's name on it. It will be cherished by the grieving parents.
- Send a card when you learn of the death of a child. They will hold onto these keepsakes for a long time.
- If you don't know what to say, be honest. Chances are, they don't either. Simply knowing that they have someone patiently there with them can make all the difference.
- If this person begins to cry, don't feel badly like it's your fault. Grieving parents may cry a lot, and it's not your fault. Just hold their hand or (if you're in public together) take them some quiet place to allow them to calm down.
- Not all grief looks the same. While some people will grieve the loss of their child by crying, not all will cry in front of you. That does not mean that they are "better" or "over it." They will never be over it.
- Grief is uncomfortable. If you begin to feel uncomfortable around parents, stay anyway.
- Ask, "Can I help you with anything?" If they says no, ask again. Then ask again.
- Figure out, through friends or family members, what sort of help the grieving parents need and do it without being asked. Grief may make it very difficult to manage even the simplest tasks - they might not even know what they need.
- Let the parent(s) talk about their lost child.
- Share stories about the baby or child.
- There is no time-line for grief.
- When you visit, bring a bag of groceries, throw in a load of laundry, and clean up the kitchen. Daily responsibilities are extremely difficult while in the throes of grief.
- It's okay if you only have fifteen minutes to stop by and visit. Do it anyway.
- If you've agreed to help, DO IT. Find someone else to do it, if you can't manage it. Asking for help is REALLY hard, so if you're asked, HONOR it.
- Follow the lead of the parents. Discuss what they want. If they go to those places, you can discuss those things, but don't try to steer it there. Sometimes, the grieving parents may want to talk about their child and the unfairness of it all, and other times they may want to hear funny stories or talk about reality TV.
- Address the unfairness. People often worry about addressing how awful the situation is, but the parents want to hear that people get what it's like for them. The parents feel alone when they don't think people understand how awful this is. Saying things like, "This is the worst thing. I am so sorry and sad that it had to happen to you and your child," helps.
- Food is very helpful. The last thing a person wants to do when mourning is worry about eating. There are always people around after a death, and the last thing you

want to think about is feeding them. A gift of food also tells the parents they are loved.

- If you're financially able to, send some money to the grieving parents. The cost of a funeral for a child is high, and is often (especially if the loss of the child is not expected) not planned for.
- Say or express something you never have before. If you have never told the person that you love them, come right out and tell them that you love them. If you've never held their hand, hold their hand. Give hugs. These expressions mean a lot.

**Do not be afraid to take initiative.**

- Be there for this person. Call, email, text. Tell them they don't have to respond. Let them know you are thinking of them, and their child, all the time. Don't drop away after the funeral – that's when they'll need you the most.
- Be the kind of friend that you would want to have.
- Remember the living children. When visiting, bring a toy or something you think the child would like.
- Try to remember the dates that are associated with the loss. They may include:
  - a) The anniversary of the child's death.
  - b) The date of the miscarriage.
  - c) The due-date of the miscarriage.
  - d) The birthday of the lost child.
  - e) Your friend's birthday
  - f) Holidays like Mother's Day and Father's Day.
- Make a donation to a specific cause or charity in honor of the parent's lost child.
- Be patient with them…they need it.

**What NOT to Do**

- Don't be afraid of intruding. You're not.
- Don't be afraid of offering practical help. This person probably has no idea what he or she needs, so take some initiative.
- Don't avoid or ignore the grieving parents. They are already grieving a loss, and losing a friend or loved one only compounds it.
- Don't leave when you become uncomfortable. It will only make your friend feel worse - guilty about their grief.
- Don't avoid talking to your friend because you don't know what to say.
- Do not say, "It is for the best," even if you believe it.

- Don't shirk on promises - if you've agreed to do something for the grieving family, failing at your responsibilities will feel like a bigger slap in the face.
- Don't be hurt if the grieving parents say something mean or hurtful. They're not quite themselves, which means they lash out. Be patient.
- Religion is a potentially explosive way to comfort. Unless you absolutely know 100% the person will be comforted by mentions of faith, don't go there. Religion is a very complicated thing in the wake of a child's death, and they may be angry at God or confused as to how to incorporate the death of a child into the religion that they have known to have their best interests in mind.
- Even if the grieving parents are intensely religious, they may be having a crisis of faith in the wake of a child's death, and they could be angered/saddened by mention of religion.
- Especially stay away from, "God wanted her more than you," or "God needed her more." I don't care if it is the all-powerful creator of the universe, you don't tell *any* Mama that anyone wants her baby more than she does.
- So many people hate seeing their loved one in such pain and want to fix it. Consequently, they start talking about how you have to move on, that you will see them again, the child is with God, it will get better in time, etc. - all things they think will "fix it." Don't try to do this.
- Don't be afraid to bring up the lost child - the grieving parents will already be thinking of their child.
- If the parent doesn't want to discuss their lost child or their feelings, accept that and move on to another topic.
- Don't say, "I know how you feel," because you do not. It minimizes the grief and grieving they're going through.
- Don't say, "I don't know how you do it." They are doing it because he or she has to.
- Don't mention silver linings. That feels condescending and rude.
- Don't put a time-table on grief. No one knows how long it will take to grieve the loss of a child, so don't expect that this parent will simply "get over it" in a specific period of time. They won't.
- Don't refer to the child in impersonal ways - instead, use the child's name. It may feel uncomfortable to you, but it will remind this parent that the world has not, in fact, forgotten their lost child.
- Don't forget about the siblings of the lost child. Not only have they lost a brother or sister, they've lost their parents during the grieving process.
- Never discount your gut. If this person seems to be suicidal or is beginning to isolate, seek professional help.

- Don't forget the anniversary dates - almost no one remembers the second anniversary of a child's death. This makes parents feel as though the world has forgotten their child.
- Don't be afraid to show emotion. Many people feel they have to be strong for the people that they are ministering to, that they can't cry or show emotion. You can be strong AND be emotional. If tears come, don't fight them. This shows this parent that you, too, are crushed and sad and lost.

# ~ DIVORCE ~

"...but God hath called us to peace" 1 Corinthians 7:15

## DIVORCE...DIVORCEE' STYLE

"What God hath joined together, let not man put asunder." Remember that? Every bride does. .it is a charge nestled in-between "By the power and authority invested in me by the state of wherever, I now...pronounce you husband and wife," and "I now present to you Mr. and Mrs."... you walked up the aisle, this time arm in arm with the person that you knew you would spend the rest of your life with and now you are here. What happened? Where is your happily ever after? Where is til death us do part? How do I handle this? I'm not a widow(er), I'm a divorcee'!!!!!

Although it may seem like a fairly common occurrence, 1 out of every 2 marriages statistically speaking end in divorce. Divorce is almost *never* easy. At minimum, a major relationship is ending, all sorts of routines are upset, and in the midst of the stress of transition there are legal hoops to jump through before things can be resolved. Add in the volatile emotions that are frequently associated with divorce and you have a difficult situation indeed. Divorce can trigger all sorts of unsettling, uncomfortable and frightening feelings, thoughts and emotions, including grief, loneliness, depression, despair, guilt, frustration, anxiety, anger, and devastation, to name a few. There is frequently sadness and grief at the thought of the end of a significant relationship. There can be fear at the prospect of being single again, possibly for a long time (or even forever), and with having to cope with changed financial, living and social circumstances. There can be anger at a partner's stubborn obstinacy and pettiness, abuse, or outright betrayal. There can be guilt over perceived failures to have made the relationship work. There can be overwhelming depression at the thought of the seeming impossibility of being able to cope with all the changes that are required. Any and all of these emotions are enough to make people miserable, and to find them wanting to cry at 3 in the morning.

Going through a divorce, for whatever reason, can come as a shock – even if the person knew it was coming. It's a massive change and as human beings, we don't take changes very well. Yes, there are opportunities which arise out of the change but first there needs to be a processing of the feelings of rejection, grief, anxiety, panic, worry, loss of self-esteem (as sometimes the rejection experienced is taken personally) and loss of 'self' as they probably linked your self-worth to the relationship. Many feelings will arise including moodiness, upsetness, depression, anxiety, panic and insomnia. It is very hard to know how best to support someone through the roller coaster of emotions and if they are close to you, you will almost feel like you are on the roller coaster with them. You may see them going out of control and feel that something is wrong. It is not. This is what the divorce spiral looks like

In the first few weeks, it's critical for the 'soon-to-be-divorced person' to just feel their emotions. Emotions, when fully experienced, naturally evolve along the path of healing but it's often the people supporting the person being made redundant that interrupt this healing pattern.

The initial state before the cycle begins is often quite stable, at least in terms of the subsequent reaction to hearing the bad news (compared with the ups and downs to come, even if there is some variation, this is indeed a fairly stable state).
And then, in the calm of this relative paradise, a bombshell bursts...

### The *naked divorce* grieving cycle

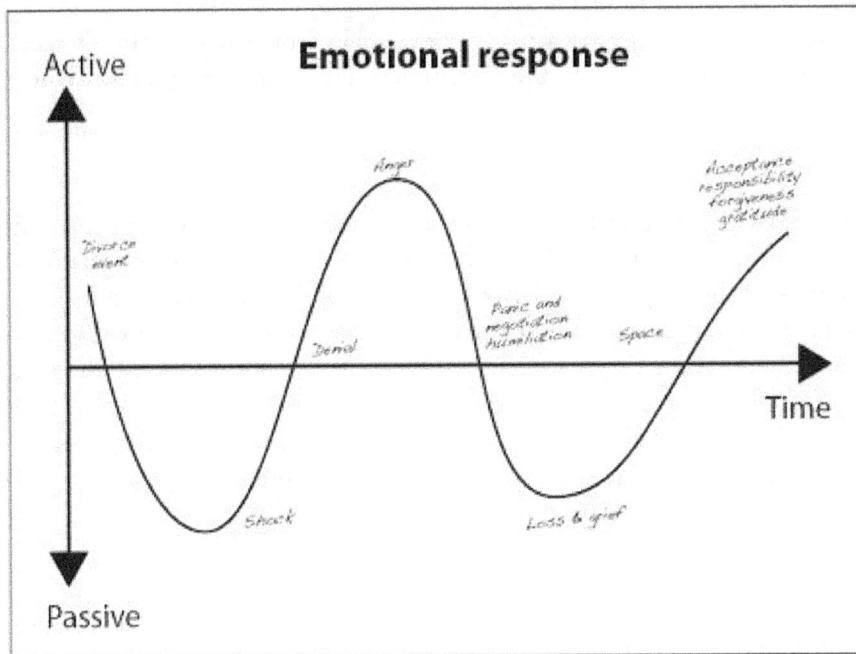

1. Denial stage: trying to avoid the inevitable.
2. Anger and betrayal stage: frustrated outpouring of bottled-up emotion.
3. Panic and negotiation stage: seeking a way out. Making deals with your ex.

4.   Humiliation, fear of failure or looking bad stage: gradually sinking into a spiral, feeling embarrassed and avoiding seeing people.
5.   Despair stage: realization that something awful is coming your way and you're strapped into the rollercoaster and helpless.
6.   Loss, grief and depression stage: a final realization of the inevitable, surrendering to the grief.
7.   Space and nothingness stage: once you have grieved and grieved, experiencing loss and pain, you're left with a feeling of nothingness. It's different to numbness because you feel very present and can notice things around you. Your senses are heightened. You may also find that you cannot cry anymore. You experience an emotional vacuum.
8.   Acceptance stage: seeking realistic solutions and finally finding the way forward, it's not a feeling of resignation. It's a feeling of profound understanding of the way things are and the way things are not.
9.   Responsibility and forgiveness stage: taking responsibility for where you may have caused cracks in the relationship and contributed to its subsequent breakdown and divorce. Forgiving your ex and yourself for any failings during the relationship is a critical part of true and real healing.
10. Gratitude stage: transformational experience. Learning from your divorce and seeing positives and negatives from the experience. This stage completes the healing

If the end of a marriage is contested or involves disputes over money or property, it becomes even *more* difficult. If the relationship involves children, and especially if there are issues around child custody, the world might just feel like it's wobbling on its axis. Going through a divorce may upset everything a person knows to be true, and without the help and support of friends and family, a person can find him or herself in a devastating rut.

Learning to be alone for the first time in a long time can be extraordinarily lonely and depressing. Being part of a couple becomes a way of life, and adjusting to the newness of being a single, learning to do things alone, can be absolutely devastating, especially in the early stages of a divorce.

What this person in your congregation and or community needs, above all else is this: **_knowing they have someone in their corner._** This is not to be confused with taking sides. It is simply to have a full well and safe place in their life.

## What You Can Do To Help

- Acknowledge that this is a terrible situation. Because it is. Sure, there can be a lot of good that comes of the divorce, but the short-term reality is that this is a terrible thing that has happened/ is happening. So tell them that you do, in fact, understand.
- Listen. Listen. Listen. And then listen some more.
- Try to encourage this person to find and attend a local support group for divorcée's if there is not one available at your church. The comfort of those who are going through exactly the same situation is invaluable.
- Attend court dates, weddings, or funerals with this person when to do so will not be interpreted as taking sides. As someone who is used to having a built in "plus one," this will go a long way toward making them feel comfortable.
- Remind this person that they are not a bad person - just stuck in a bad situation. Sometimes the guilt of divorce can be crushing.
- The grief from a divorce may take a long time to overcome - remind this person of this, if he or she feels as though it's "taking too long."
- Love unconditionally. You don't have to approve of this choice to love them.
- Hug this person often - they were used to being hugged by their spouse often. They're probably missing that physical touch.
- Especially during the early days, remind them to breathe - and focus on one day at a time.
- Help them sit down and review household bills to figure out their expenses. Often, this simple task can seem insurmountable as they go from a dual income family to a single income. Even more devastating, going from a dependent spouse to having to find a means to support herself.
- Help fill the freezer with ready-to-eat meals. Grief often makes it hard to practice self-care, which can include proper meals.
- Help to go with this person to find a place to live if the divorce is leaving them looking for a home.
- This person may want to revisit what happened and try to piece together where it all went wrong. You won't have the answers. They won't have the answers. This is okay. Just listen.
- Offer to be a companion for night's out or dinners in to ease your friend into their new single lifestyle.
- If you offer to help, **commit** to it. The last thing a person losing their partner needs is *another* person bailing on them.
- Hold off on giving specific advice.
- If you ARE asked "what should I do about (insert item here)?" present both the pros and cons of the situation to help this person see the full picture. Remind them that it is their decision, not yours, and that he/she needs to what's in their best interest and the best interest of the child(ren).

- Help document the details - things to tell the lawyer and/or counselor, items your friend will need when they move out, grocery lists, kids activities, whatever.

**If there are minor children involved:**

- Keep the children out of it as much as possible.
- Keep the talk about the divorce, the lawyers, the ex, to a minimum.
- Don't ask the children for information about the other parent. If they bring it up, fine, but don't go searching for it.
- Offer to take the children while this person is dealing with the attorneys or the courts.
- Offer to take the children if you feel that the person a break.
- Watch for signs of depression or anxiety, both in this person and in the children.

## What You Should NOT Do

- Don't bash their ex. Even if it seems super obvious that this person is better off without their ex, don't rub it in - it's just going to make them feel worse. This person already feels bad enough - hearing how you never liked the ex won't make them friend feel any better.
- Don't choose sides. If you're friends with both partners, it's really hard to be friends with both and extra hard not to choose sides. What you need to do is just listen to what either side has to say. Hold your tongue if one partner behaves poorly and keep your opinions to yourself.
- Don't push this person into doing things if they want to be alone. People going through a divorce need some time to be alone, so try to respect their wishes as best as you can. Remember, if you're happily married, a newly divorced person may want to avoid you, simply because it hurts to have the reminder that other people are still in happy relationships. Don't take it personally. You simply may not be the right person to help at this time.
- Don't assume that offering help gives you the right to voice an opinion.
- Don't share the details of the divorce or separation with others.
- Don't use clichés. They come across as preachy and condescending.
- Don't rent happy romantic comedies to watch with them is this is something that you do.
- Don't fix this person up on a date. When he or she is ready to date, you'll know it.

- Don't judge. It may be really hard, especially if choosing divorce is something you believe to be a mistake, but remember that you do not know what goes on behind closed doors.
- Don't offer advice unless asked. Unless, of course, the kids are suffering or there are serious pressing issues with money.
- Don't ever - EVER - give legal advice. That is for a divorce attorney alone to provide. You don't know all of the legal ins and outs of the situation, even if you've been divorced before.
- If you're in a new relationship or a happy one, don't rub it in. Use discretion if you're in a relationship. That doesn't mean you have to stop living, just try to be considerate and sensitive for a while. Again, this may not be the person in the congregation that you need to minister too. It's alright not to tackle every need that you see. The key is to be effective in the ministering that you do.
- Don't lend money unless you're okay with not getting it back. Finances are strained for those in a divorce. They don't need the strain of reminders that they owe someone else money.
- Don't become offended if the person doesn't act grateful for your help. When someone is overcome with grief, it may be a day-to-day struggle to survive, let alone be able to practice thankfulness.

## HEY, I'M NOT A VILLIAN...I JUST NEEDED OUT

"I didn't wake up this morning and say, 'hey I want a divorce'," "People don't know what I did, how hard I tried, the part that wasn't mine, yet I am the villain because I filed the papers" "It took both of us to create this mess yet because I filed the paperwork I wear the scarlet letter" "I can't believe how incredibly cruel people can be especially in the church. People who used to speak to me don't speak to me anymore. People who used to go out with me and fellowship with me don't fellowship with me anymore. I'm invited out of events instead of to events. Why? Because I chose to stop hurting?"

These are actual statements from actual people who chose to file for divorce. They are the forgotten victim on the divorce continuum. It seems that everyone wants to rally around the spouse who was divorced, not knowing what precipitated the divorce. People are surrounding the children who are now a part of a broken home because of the divorce. However, people tend to shun the partner who dissolved the marriage. It is as if somehow because they took the steps to end the pain, they took the steps to regain some sense of normalcy, peace, self-esteem and happiness they are now and forever labeled "the bad guy/girl" When we really, really look at this thing called divorce, who actually knows what led to the death of the marriage? Three people, the husband, the wife and the Lord. So why is it that we automatically flock to the one "who was left" and not the one "who left?"

For some reason we feel as though the decision to divorce was taken likely, but the reverse is true. Just as marriage should not be entered into lightly, the same is true for divorce. Many grapple with the decision for years prior to making the decision that this is the best choice. Ruth Chang offers a perspective that I have found consistent with my experience marriage counseling with people who are grappling with this hard choice. She illustrates the fact that what often makes a choice between two options so difficult is that there is no clear better choice. For example, As Ruth explains, (and I am choosing a very simplistic example here to make the point), if my choice is between a doughnut for breakfast and a high fiber cereal and I place very high value on my health, the choice is easy. If, however, I equally care about taste and health, even this insignificant choice can become difficult. Applying each interest leads to a different outcome, potentially leaving me at a stalemate. I could make the cereal healthier by adding flaxseeds or the doughnut better tasting by adding a filling, and none of this would change my dilemma. There is still no clear better choice since I still equally care about health and taste.

Now let's apply this to the marriage situation. Let's assume I value seeing my kids everyday (which I get to do if I stay married). I value being happy (which I am not feeling in my marriage). I value security (which I perceive I will have if I stay married). I love my home (which I will probably lose if I get divorced). Even if we could attribute numeric value amounts to all of these choices (which we can't), the pull between the happiness and the other factors would still feel unresolvable.

Additionally, there is also the problem of uncertainty. How do I know if I will be happier if I get divorced? How will I know there is true security if I stay married? How do I know if my spouse will change and things will improve? Or get worse? What if this is a speed bump and not a road closure and I misread the sign? What we default to, is to thinking that there really is one right choice and that we, because of some personal failing or inadequacy, are just incapable of figuring it out. Since we could be wrong, many people take the safer route or choose the status quo for fear of making a big mistake.

This is a difficult decision to make and difficult decisions are not a test of how smart or wise you are but rather an opportunity to actively write the story of your life. Difficult decisions, serve as forks in the road that enable us to look back at the path we have traveled, recognize that there are options for moving forward, and then take an active role in choosing who we want to be. In choosing, we can stand FOR something and declare, "This is who I am." If we don't actively choose, we become *drifters* and allow the world to dictate the unfolding of our life.

Now that the choice has been made and the person has finally gathered up the courage to actually say to their spouse that they want a divorce, the whirlwind begins. It is not as if the issues come as a surprise. There have been comments, conversations, frustrations expressed and feelings all along. It is just NOW many times when love has died and or a boundary has been breached that cannot be repaired the other spouse reacts as if this is the first that they have heard of it. Now they want therapy, now they want to work on reconciliation. When the other cried out for help it was not take seriously. Hind sight is 20-20. Now the news is out. The marriage is over and divorce in impending or recently happened. Society reacts as if this was the fairytale marriage, the spouse divorced was perfect and the one filing is the big bad wolf. Let's be honest readers…We really do not know what has happened.

Let's look at some more statistics: 3% of all divorces are the result of an extramarital affair. 7% of divorces are the result of domestic Violence. 2 % of divorce is the result of a trauma in the family such as the death of a child that caused so much strain the marriage couldn't last and 3 % of divorces are the result of a spouse being incarcerated and 5 % of marriages are due to substance abuse. This means that 80% of all divorces are because we were not good stewards over the marriage until we felt it slipping through our fingers. We took one another for granted. We minimized their concerns and complaints. We felt that since it was not a problem for us that it should not be a problem for our spouse. We in a sense worked very hard at killing our love and now we want to vilify the filing spouse instead of taking responsibility for our part in the death of the marriage. What we need to understand is that in a divorce, there are two (2) victims. This filer in your community and congregation is hurting too, they are in need of love and ministry too, he/she, needs you too.

- The leaving spouse usually has initial feelings of freedom mingled with guilt.
- Even though the divorce was already thought out, often long in advance of the actual separation. Sometimes, for the spouse who left, they may have initially spent years trying to save a cold marriage and eventually gave up. For this person, filing for divorce is just a formality because in their heart, the marriage died long ago.
- For the spouse who left, the pain may be immediate. The pain also may not be immediate but can come up years later in the form of deep-seeded guilt and regret, manifesting itself in other relationships.
- That person most likely is struggling with low self-worth. Remember, their marriage has failed as well.

## WHAT CAN I DO

- Don't turn your back on this person simply because you don't agree with their choice.
- Don't take sides. Sometimes we take sides in our trying to protect people's feelings. For example we will invite the divorcee' and not invite the leaving spouse for fear of making either or both of them uncomfortable. Invite both or neither. Give them both the opportunity to accept or decline. You are not responsible for their decisions.
- Don't assume that you know and or understand the reasons for the divorce. Many times the leaving spouse will not vilify the divorced spouse.
- Be a shoulder, ear and safe place for the leaving spouse. There is a lot in there that they are holding in and need to process.
- Continue the relationship when possible. They left their marriage, they didn't leave their love and relationship with you.
- Understand that being a leaving spouse is a lonely place to be. Everyone needs someone. Consider being that "someone" for the leaving spouse in your congregation and or community.

## CHILDREN OF DIVORCE

Researchers have filled volumes studying and analyzing the effect of divorce on children. Studies examining the children of divorce have found that most suffer a sense of loss and that the feelings can manifest in many different ways, depending on the children's ages and unique personalities, as well as on how the parents handle the divorce.

Younger children may regress in areas such as sleeping and toilet training, or throw more tantrums. School-age and teenage children may show symptoms of depression, rebel against discipline, or change their eating and sleeping habits.

Recent research has shown that adult children of divorce have higher divorce rates than adults with parents in stable marriages -- and even those who remain married report they are have less trust for their spouses than people whose parents have remained married.

Before going any further let's spend a little time with Joanie:

> When I was 8 years old, my parents divorced. I have no memory of the day we moved away, and the following nine months are a blur. I don't remember the

drive to another city, moving in with relatives, starting school, or my new teacher. I have one vague recollection of a teacher praising my schoolwork, but she has no name or face.

In contrast, I can remember the smallest details of my life before the separation. I recall the gray swirled wallpaper in my bedroom, and the green and white gingham dress that my Aunt Dorothy gave to me for my birthday. I have a vivid recollection of my brother's crib complete with teeth marks, and my treasured chalkboard where I would "teach" my dolls. The Tide® Box was stored on the bathroom windowsill, and our brown sofa was plaid. And a small, white radio that sat on top of the refrigerator entertained me as I washed dishes.

Twenty-three years later, I found myself in a pastor's office weeping. I had just quit a high-stress job with a boss who was impossible to please. Instead of experiencing relief, I was overwhelmed with despair. When the pastor questioned the reason for my anxiety, I replied, "I don't know. All I know is that I'm eight years old again, and I can't do one thing right." I was as perplexed as he was to hear those words come out of my mouth.

As the conversation continued, it became painfully clear that this little girl, with a memory loss, believed she was the reason for her parents' divorce. The torture of that conviction was too burdensome for my tiny mind to endure. So I forgot. Thirty-one years later, sitting in that office, the truth unfolded. The shame and trauma of my parents' divorce haunted my life and influenced my decisions. And I never even knew it.

Children and divorce is a complex subject and there are no easy answers. However, it's imperative for parents to learn that they play a pivotal role in minimizing the trauma children experience and experience it they do.

- **Most kids will initially go into a form of denial when their parents separate.** They think, "This is temporary, my parents will get back together." Even years later, many kids still dream about their parents reuniting, which is usually one reason why they resist a parent's remarriage.
- **Most children will internalize this divorce feeling that in some way it is their fault.**
- **Children grieve.** Children are unable to communicate grief in the same manner as adults. Therefore, they may be sad, angry, frustrated, or depressed, but cannot express it.
- **Children are not resilient, they are plastic and each change that is being made is reshaping them in some way!** Understand that the more uprooting this child has

experienced and the more changes that they have endured as a result of this divorce is changing them little by little. This includes moving into a new home, starting a new school, changing churches, or new friends, etc. It emotionally harms children when parents use them as spies, mediators, or informants. They feel trapped in the middle of a no-win situation.

- **Allow your child to love the other parent and extended family.** They didn't get divorced from their mother or father—you did. Children cannot choose between parents. They love both parents It too both parents to create this child, yet in a very real sense children feel that they have to choose one and spy on the other.
- **Children lose trust.** In an age-appropriate manner, and without gory details, tell the truth. The number one reason kids blame themselves for their parent's divorce is because they were not told the truth.
- **Children personalize the things stated about their other parent. Don't belittle the other parent.** When a parent bashes or criticizes the other parent it can emotionally destroy a child's self-worth. "If dad is a no-good loser, I must be one too." "If mom is a tramp, that's what I'll become."
- **Children want to see their other parent. They love Mommy or Daddy** The children who do the best after a divorce are those who have a strong relationship with both biological parents. Therefore, do not withhold visitation unless the child is being neglected or in danger.

This is what you will see in the pew or community. This is what these children look like. Why? Because divorce can be a painful and confusing time in a family's life. It's normal for children to experience a roller coaster of emotions — from sadness, loss, hurt and anger, to confusion, guilt, abandonment and withdrawal. Every child manages in her own way and heals at her own pace. However, there are a number of ways that you can help make coping during this difficult period of transition a little easier.

## 1. Provide Love and Reassurance

Reassure the child(ren) that both parents love them. Help them to understand that the divorce is not their fault. Explain that the love for a parent towards a child is a different type of love that the love between a husband and a wife. Children will often think, "If mommy stopped loving daddy, then will she will stop loving me?" and vice versa It's important for children to understand that their parents will never stop loving them. Making a small photo book of your child from birth to present, writing a short caption underneath each picture stating why she is such a blessing in your life. Include a couple of milestones or memorable events that took place in each year of your child's life.

## 2. Encourage Communication

Not only is it important that you give this child accurate information about the divorce (i.e. mommy and daddy will not be living together but they still love you), but you need to give these children ample opportunity to talk about how she's feeling and to ask questions about the changes that are happening in the family. Find creative ways to help the child deal with her feelings. Keep in mind that some children just need some time and space to sort things out for herself, so try to avoid forcing her to talk about the divorce if she's not up for it. Just having the chance to "hang out" with someone who cares, or jot things down in a journal can be positive coping tools for children. Ways you can facilitate dialogue include:

- One-on-one time: Make sure to carve out a few minutes from your schedule routinely to find out about the child's day, or week and to be emotionally available to listen without interruptions.
- Peer interaction: Peers can be powerful sounding boards and supporters. Help child stay connected to trusted friends during this time, and consider helping with "play dates" with friends now that mommy or daddy may not have the time to keep this up.
- Feelings journal/scrapbook: This is a child's personal keepsake and can include drawings, journal entries, photos, and mementos, anything that reflects how the child is feeling at a given time. Encourage the child to add to it often. She can choose to keep it private or she can share it with you; the decision is hers. If she does share her scrapbook with you, use it as a conversation starter, particularly with an introverted or withdrawn child, to get a read on how she's really doing.

## 3. Validate feelings

Children need to know that their feelings are normal, and that in time, they will feel better. Find safe and acceptable outlets for the children to get her aggressions out and help her channel those feelings into positive activities. Help them to get to Sunshine Band, Purity or what other activities are for the children at your church. Some other potential outlets are:

- Sports such as martial arts, soccer, or kickboxing
- Quiet zone – Give the child(ren) a comforting place where she can feel calm, away from the noise and distractions of the rest of the turmoil of their home house. Sitting in a quiet space and squeezing a stress ball can help dissipate tantrums and relax younger children.
- Art projects – Let the child get good and messy with finger paints. Give older children carpenter's tools to build something. Build a birdhouse or a toy chest together and let your child paint it. Give the child clay to knead, mold and sculpt.

When you can visibly see that the child is experiencing a powerful emotion, try asking her about it. You might say, "It seems like you are feeling upset right now. Is there anything I can do to help you?"

Older kids especially can be very angry and act out or blame parents. In that case, Listen but reinforce that it is ok to feel hurt and upset by the situation but it is never ok to be disrespectful to either parent.

## 4. Help Keep Things as Amicable as Possible

What makes children suffer the most is hostility between parents. While it may be easier said than encourage parents if you can maneuver this correctly, to attempt to me a little more civil in front of the child. If tensions are high, communicate by email or hand-written notes rather than in person or on the telephone.

- Divorce is not about playing tug of war for a child's affection or using the child to spy on the other parent. Be the safe place where the child can share the happy times on a visitation with the non-custodial parent without having to feel guilty for having a good time. Many times after a divorce children will not talk about visits because they feel guilty or because of the anger and intensity of negative feelings that the parent is dealing with. You can be the one that this child can laugh at and enjoy the time with the other parent.
- Never bad mouth the non-custodial parent regardless to how you feel about the divorce. This is about the child.
- It is important not to use your child as a messenger. Communicate directly with the other parent, and avoid attacking words. Brady recommends using non-confrontational statements such as, "I'm hearing that…" or "Johnny reports that…and I wanted to talk to you about it."

## 5. Be Reliable

If you say you're going to pick spend time with this child do it and, be punctual. When you don't you can cause stress and worry, and make the child feel even more rejected and unimportant.

## 6. Remember That the Child is a Child

- Help parent understand that they shouldn't turn their child into a confidant. Complaining to a child and using a child for emotional support will make her suffer unnecessarily. This child needs you to be their advocate.
- While children of divorce do tend to become adult more quickly, it's not fair to treat them like adults. Saying things like, "You're the man of the house now" puts too much pressure on kids.

DR. PATRICIA LOTT

# ~ FAMILIES OF PRISONERS ~

*"But Mary Kept these things and Pondered them in her heart" Lk 2:19*

As of 2009, the United States had the highest incarceration rate in the world. Roughly 743 people of every 100,000 are incarcerated. With over 2.3 million people in prison in 2013, there are a *lot* of friends and family members on the outside with concerns about their loved one in jail.

**The family is not guilty; anyone can have a family member go to prison.**

Many relatives of prisoners have said that the grief they felt when their family member went to prison was similar to the death of a loved one. Even though a prisoner can still be visited and spoken to on the phone sometimes, the loss for the family is a very real one.

However, the process of grieving that loss is quite difficult for prisoners' families. When someone dies, neighbors, friends and family will usually be very supportive and understanding. The same support is generally not offered to the families of prisoners, and they feel that they are being judged alongside the offender.

Funerals, laying of flowers, and other rituals associated with death all help bereaved relatives to express their emotions, find meaning in their experience, and ultimately to move on, with the support of the community. There are no rituals to help prisoners' families cope with their loss. Their pain many times is not regarded as 'legitimate' in the same way.

This lack of social support can make it difficult for them to express their sorrow openly. As a result, families often hide their feelings from others and try to cope on their own. Not expressing sadness and grief can mean that it is difficult to move on and can lead to health issues such as anxiety and depression. It is important to have the opportunity to talk about what they are going through and how they feel and ways to deal with your experiences.

## Guilt by association

Families of prisoners have been called the 'invisible victims of crime'. Stereotypes of prisoners and widespread fear of crime and criminals can also lead people to discriminate against the families of prisoners. In the case of a trial attracting media attention or sexually based, for instance, judgment and fear within the local community and even among family and friends may be strong.

As the family member of a prisoner, people are given a hard time for wanting to maintain a relationship with someone sentenced for a crime. It can be difficult for extended family to deal with their own shame and fear of being judged by others. This may cause friends and relatives to avoid contact with them as well as their imprisoned partner. This is because family and friends can feel so ashamed of the prisoner, that they assume others will judge them and so, they isolate themselves. These children become the unintended victims of this sudden, unexplained disappearance of support from friends and family.

## The Forgotten Victims

Many families with a loved one in prison experience economic hardship, especially if the incarcerated person was a primary wage-earner of the household. Spouses lose a co-parent to jail, and find themselves raising children alone. It goes without saying that the impact of having a parent incarcerated on the children is enormous. Children of inmates in jail are at a greater risk of being incarcerated in the future. As if this weren't enough, families with an incarcerated loved one experience social stigmas in their community because their loved one is in jail. Sad to say, many of these spouses and children have family and friends who don't agree with them standing by their loved one, therefore they find themselves without any support."

Many family members of inmates feel that they are also being punished for the crime committed by their loved one. It's common for them to feel guilty for the actions of their loved ones. They find themselves excluded from certain financial services like insurance or bank loans due to their loved one's criminal past. Depending on the nature of the crime and the publicity surrounding it, members of the community may lash out at the family in the place of the offender. Children may be bullied for being "different."

Family members often find themselves intentionally isolating themselves from friends and neighbors who simply don't understand what it's like, in order to protect themselves. 45% of inmates lose contact with their loved ones while they are incarcerated. Many families find themselves avoiding the subject of their loved one, pretending that individual doesn't exist, because the subject is too painful or frustrating.

This is a family in crisis. Supporting someone in prison causes increased levels of financial insecurity due to:

- o The loss of one income
- o The loss of the main caregiver for the children

- o Increased costs of maintaining family contact, such as providing goods and money for the prisoner, travelling to prisons and potential loss of or moving from the family home
- o Managing debts that are left behind such as court costs and outstanding bills.

They must decide whether to spend the money for visitations and essential supplies for their family member or taking care of responsibilities at home. If she/he misses too many Sunday services because of travel and visitations they are labeled unfaithful. They deal with so many stressful situations surrounding a simple visit with the loved on.  Just listen to the voice of a wife whose husband was incarcerated for 10 years: with spunk and thoughtfulness, Bessie says

> "I send a package to William every Christmas, and usually a few to guys whose families aren't involved or can't afford it.  Christmas comes once a year, but visitation is a regular expense—especially since the prison is miles away. Inmates are often transferred between prisons based on capacity, custody level, medical needs or special programming—all of which take precedence over placing them near relatives. During his term, William has been moved through more than a half-dozen counties."

To reach some of these places, Bessie reports paying $50 in travel costs each weekend—plus the price of phone calls, books, sneakers and a weekly allowance so William can buy basic items such as soap and toothpaste. "I dare not try to sit down and count up how much money I've spent over the years because I would probably pass out," she says.

Now let's hear a word from Linda, "It's like the system has no consideration and no concern for how the family is affected. My brother has been in and out of prison for the past two decades. Visitation as a stressful, emotional event. Once, my mother and I arrived late due to traffic and were blocked from visitation. We were one or two minutes late and they shut the gates on us. My heart was broken, my mother sat outside the wall on the floor crying out of her soul. The guards had us removed from the prison for disturbing the peace and unlawful assembly. It was heart-wrenching to us and my brother because he was expecting us."

This is just a small glimpse into the life of the family of prisoners. How you may ask can we help them. The first thing you can do is to remember that the incarceration is not your Sister/brother's fault. Then help them to realize that this is their family member's incarceration and *not theirs nor is it their fault*. No matter what they tell themselves, there is **nothing** that they could have done to help their loved one avoid this situation. Going to jail is a result of your loved one's actions alone.

So….How can you help?  In this situation with this population the best thing that you can do is listen? The next best thing that you can do is to be there for them making things as normal as possible for this family in crises. There will be many emotional times. Encourage them to talk it out. To feel it and then pray **with** them. Depending on their situation and the type of relationship that they have with the individual who is now incarcerated, it's important that they develop some coping strategies to help them deal with the incarceration in a productive way. Above all else, make certain that their coping strategies help them, and their loved one **without** compromising their own well-being. Below is a list of discussion starter for families of prisoners to help them to begin developing their coping strategies

- Help them to remember that it is their loved one who is in jail not them. When you see or hear the self-blame say something like, "Remember that your loved one is responsible for their choices in life, choices that led them to jail, not you."

- I can see that this is a very emotional time for you and your family as you attempt to carry on alone. It might be hard but it will help a lot if you take some time now to make decisions as to how much emotional support you can provide your loved one in jail. *How often are you willing to visit? How many times per week or month do you plan on talking via telephone? How often do you plan on writing letters?* Set these benchmarks ahead of time and stick to your guns. Don't commit more than you are capable of providing.

- I can see that your loved one's incarceration is very financially challenging for you and your children. A way to help alleviate the burden is to decide how much financial support you're willing to provide, and how often. Be mindful of your budget and what you can afford. Don't feel bad if you can't spare anything.

- It is OK to need to speak with someone about how all of this is affecting you and your family. I am here for you. You can talk to me. I will listen and I will care and I will help as I can.

- Encourage them to continue to live their lives and work on their own personal plans and goals. ***Remind them that they should be their first priority.*** This is not turning their back on their loved one but it is taking care of what their loved one has left behind. That is the number one priority!

- Help them to understand that their family's normal routine (on a day-to day-level and also during special occasions or holidays) can and *must* continue as normal. Encourage them to try to find ways to involve your jailed loved one if possible.

- If your Sister/Brother or the children see or hear something on the news about prison life that upsets them, remind them that their loved one will be safe if they make good decisions and lifestyle choices while incarcerated. Suggest that they avoid watching television shows or movies that might trigger anxiety and make them upset. Then *immediately* PRAY with them until the Spirit of Fear is lifted up off of them.

- You may hear that this person's incarcerated loved one has acted out in various ways during contact with them, by acting manipulative or controlling. Remind them that their loved one may simply be afraid of losing them and is feeling disconnected from their former life. 45% of all inmates lose contact with their family members while in prison, and this may be something that they're afraid of. Keep this in mind and reassure them, but make sure to stress that they not allow themselves to compromise their own self-respect.
- Strongly suggest that they not hold on to unnecessary obligations or responsibilities for their incarcerated loved one. If it's something that can be replaced later and adds undo burden on suggest that they let it go.

Lastly, anticipate stressful times for the family members of prisoners and prepare for them. These stressful times usually include the following: when the loved one is arrested, transferred, reviewed for parole, and released. Being mindful of these times will help you to be more sensitive to the changes of mood and behavior as well as position you better to be there as a support for the families during these times.

In closing I would like to submit a poem that was inspired as I watched what a spouse of a prisoner in the body of Christ went through. It is my prayer that it helps us to think a little more about our voiced opinions and hidden feelings toward the family members of prisoners.

## THE FORGOTTEN VICTIM
Dedicated to SVT from Me

"That's her there! Her hubby's inside!"
"How can she stand by him?" a preacher cried!
"I'd throw away the lock and key!'"
"That husband of hers should never be free!"

"That woman can do so much better than him!"
"I'd throw all his letters away in the bin!"
"Just what can he offer now he's locked away?"
"A complete waste of space!" a sister shouted that day.

"That's the one there! Her husband's inside!"
"He's scum of the earth!" a neighbors implied!
"If I was her, well I'd meet someone else!
"Not wasting my life to be left on the shelf!"

"That woman's been left to cope with the shame."
"It was all over the papers! And gave out his name"
"He's useless! A criminal! Bring back the rope!"
"He'll do it again! For him there's no hope!"

That man you condemn has a child and a wife
A Mom and a Dad who have given him life!
What would you do if this happened to yours?
Deny all your love and close all the doors?

Do you honestly think I'd sink to a level
And just turn my back and deem him a devil?
Yes! He's done wrong and is serving his time
And No! I do not agree with his crime.

"That woman" you point at, yes it is me
I was born with a name, as I'm human you see!
I'm innocent! just in case you forgot
And love him whether you like it or not!

I've had the abuse, the comments and more
It's nothing I haven't heard all before
I mean no offense when I say this to you
I'm a victim as well- A forgotten one too.

# ~ *GLBTQ COMMUNITY* ~

*"The LORD hath appeared of old unto me, saying, Yea, I have loved thee with an everlasting love: therefore with lovingkindness have I drawn thee" Jeremiah 31:3*

***Author's Note: I want it to be perfectly clear that I in no way condone or agree with the lifestyle choices in this chapter. I am fully aware of what scripture says concerning this matter. However, I will never, under any circumstance, take scripture out of context and use it as an "unjust balance" in order to justify bad behavior by the believing community. ***

This has got to be by far the most difficult chapter in the book to write. Perhaps it is because the emotions, judgments and at times down right hatred that runs on both sides of the issue. I had to rewrite certain parts of this book two days after my presentation at a workshop where this topic of discussion came up. I was horrified at the entire way that Christians were conducting themselves on the subject of homosexuals and lesbians. I found myself a committee of one…so I thought. At the conclusion of the workshop the floor was opened for a panel discussion with all of the presenters. There were so many questions concerning this subject and with each answer given by the presenters there was nothing to help change the thinking and feeling and behaving of what I was seeing. I felt the Lord telling me to maintain my stance in the face of this hatred and opposition and to remain in a place of compassion. I listened to scripture being twisted and invented to justify so many things and I simply maintained using the scripture that the Lord gave me. Then it happened. VALIDATION and CONFIRMATION came and I knew that I had heard from the Lord. An older woman in her 70's stood up and thanked me for what I had said. She shared to us an event in her life where she had found herself a single mother with nowhere to turn. She shared that she was naïve and somewhat sheltered and didn't realize that she was being groomed. She thought that she was being helped, not realizing she was being "Courted". She found herself in the middle of a lesbian relationship. Being raised in the church and a reader of the bible she knew that this was wrong and not pleasing to the Lord, but here she was. She could not talk to anyone in the church because of fear of what she saw happening in this conference today. She didn't want to be shunned or condemned and she didn't want someone stating the obvious to her. She wanted to know how to get out and help with how to get out of it. She struggled alone for 6 more months before she was free. "I had asked the Lord for years to give me the opportunity to share my testimony of how He delivered me. You would never have known my situation if I never told you. And it hurts because I know over the years so many women have been in my same situation but I never felt safe enough to share it until now. Thank you because the last part is finally over and I am finally totally free" I left that conference with four, let me repeat that four ladies that I have seen around and fellowshipped in various religious setting giving me their phone numbers and asking me to call because they are currently as of this writing struggling to be free from this lifestyle choice and had never found anyone "safe enough" to openly confess this too trustworthy enough to help them to get free. I was thanked for lifting the shame that is eating away at their guilt paralyzing them and keeping them bound. My brothers and my sister that is why this book is so important. I am happy to have this manuscript back in my hands so that I can add so much more to this chapter and I work on assignment from the Lord to help us to better draw and heal in this area.

Charles H Spurgeon once said," The Holy Spirit is to be admired, not only for the great truths which He teaches us in Scripture, but also for the wonderful manner in which those truths are balanced. The Word of God never gives too much of one thing or too little of another: it never carries a doctrine to an extreme, but tempers it with its corresponding doctrine. The truth seems to run at least in two parallel lines, it not in three, and when the Holy Spirit sets before us one line He wisely points out to us the other. The truth of divine sovereignty points out to us the other. The truth of abounding grace is qualified by human responsibility, and the teaching of abounding grace is seasoned by a remembrance of unflinching justice. Scripture gives us as it were the acid and the alkali; the rock and the oil which flows from it; the sword which cuts and the balm which heals. As our Lord sent forth His Evangelists two and two so doth He send out His truths two and two, that each may help the other, for the blessing of those who hear them."

There must be a paradigm shift in us if we are to be effective in this area. For this reason I will begin this chapter dealing with YOU….the dispenser of the compassion. For some of you this challenge may be too great. It is totally ok to never ever engage and try to help in this area. I would prefer it rather than for you to self-righteously cause more damage to this soul then is already there. Matthew 23:15 clearly states, Woe unto you, scribes and Pharisees, hypocrites! for ye compass sea and land to make one proselyte, and when he is made, ye make him twofold more the child of hell than yourselves." For the next few pages let's examine some of the thinking and feeling that this population is facing in your churches and communities.

1. ***Some sin is worse than other sin and that is why we must deal with this sin differently***. Wrong. All unrighteousness is sin: and there is a sin not unto death. 1 John 5:17. For the wages of sin is death; but the gift of God is eternal life through Jesus Christ our Lord. Romans 6:23. Behold, all souls are mine; as the soul of the father, so also the soul of the son is mine: the soul that sinneth, it shall die. Ezekiel 18:4 and , "But if ye have respect to persons, ye commit sin, and are convinced of the law as transgressors. For whosoever shall keep the whole law, and yet offend in one point, he is guilty of all. *For he that said, Do not commit adultery, said also, Do not kill. Now if thou commit no adultery, yet if thou kill, thou art become a transgressor of the law.* So speak ye, and so do, as they that shall be judged by the law of liberty. For he shall have judgment without mercy, that hath shewed no mercy; and mercy rejoiceth against judgment." James 2:9-13

2. ***God Hates Sexual Sin.*** There are more than a few things wrong with this statement. First and foremost I want to submit to you that if and I said if God hates sexual sin then you must be as aggressive and hostile toward Fornication and Adultery as you are toward Homosexuality and Lesbianism or else your argument has just bottomed out. Now let's go to the word. Proverbs 6:16-19 These six things doth the LORD hate: yea, seven are an abomination unto him: <u>A proud look</u>, <u>a lying tongue</u>, and <u>hands that shed innocent blood</u>, <u>An heart that deviseth wicked imaginations</u>, <u>feet that be swift in running to mischief</u>, <u>A false witness that speaketh lies</u>, and <u>he that soweth discord among brethren</u>.

3. ***God Destroyed Sodom and Gomorrah because of Homosesuality.*** First, there were five (5) cities involved in this biblical event not just two. Second, the scripture also points to other vices that took place not to five homosexual cities. Third what does that say of Lot's wife? If we are going to make inferences and she looked back because her heart was in Sodom was she bisexual? People find what they want in the Bible. We get into so much trouble when we try to justify our behavior by using only scripture that support what we want to say, do and feel. Ezekiel was told to "Eat the whole role" John "the whole book" Scripture is not a meal at the Old Country Buffet where we pick and choose what we want and then place our own personal spin on it. There was homosexuality in scripture prior to the Sodom account and there was homosexuality after.

Though the context of the account in question begins in Genesis 18:16 during God's conversation with Abraham by the Oaks of Mamre, the details of the encounter at Sodom itself are found in Genesis 19:4-13: Why did God destroy Sodom and Gomorrah? We can find clues not just from the Genesis account, but also from the Prophets and the New Testament books 2 Peter and Jude. These give a sense of how ancient Jewish thinkers steeped in Jewish culture understood these texts.

First, Sodom and Gomorrah were judged because of grave sin. Genesis 18:20 says, "And the Lord said, 'The outcry of Sodom and Gomorrah is indeed great, and their sin is exceedingly grave.'" Indeed, not even ten righteous people could be found in the city.

Second, it seems the judgment of these cities was to serve as a lesson to Abraham and to others that wickedness would be punished. In 2 Peter 2:6 we learn that God condemned and destroyed the cities as "an example to those who would live ungodly thereafter."

Third, peculiar qualities of the sin are described by Jude and Peter. Jude 7 depicts the activity as "gross immorality" and going after "strange flesh." Peter wrote that Lot was "oppressed by the sensual conduct of unprincipled men," and "by what he saw and heard...felt his righteous soul tormented day after day with their lawless deeds." These people were "those who indulged the flesh in its corrupt desires and despised authority" (2 Peter 2:7-10).

Fourth, there are 27 references outside of Genesis where Sodom is mentioned. It is emblematic of gross immorality, deepest depravity, and ultimate judgment.

Piecing together the biblical evidence gives us a picture of Sodom's offense. The sin of Sodom and Gomorrah was some kind of activity—a grave, ongoing, lawless, sensuous activity—that Lot saw and heard and that tormented him as he witnessed it day after day. It was an activity in which the inhabitants indulged the flesh in corrupt desires by going after strange flesh, ultimately bringing upon them the most extensive judgment anywhere in the Bible outside of the book of Revelation. So we understand this to be homosexuality. I am not attempting to be argumentative here, I just want for us to understand and acknowledge that when it comes to this account, yes there was homosexuality involved but to be fair and honest, there was a whole lot of somethings going on in these five cities all of which combined garnered this swift quick judgment of God.

4. ___The only reason Jesus didn't condemn the woman caught in the act of adultery was because her heart was ready to receive him.___ I have no idea where this came from. This writer was completely taken aback. I don't recall Jesus condemning anyone in scripture even those who crucified Him. I recall Jesus' encounter with a rich man whose heart apparently wanted to be with the followers of Christ who when told to sell all of his good and give to the poor decided that this was not really what he wanted to do. Even this man Christ did not condemn. What I like to refer to this event as is **When the law and grace came face to face.** Two things that we can take from this account that is the perfect lead in to how to minister compassion to this population in our communities and congregations are this:

   A. This woman was caught in the very act of sexual sin. The Law said that she should be stoned to death. The religious leaders were correct in the letter of the law. No one will ever dispute that. However these religious leaders forgot the fact that they themselves were also guilty under the law. For all have sinned and come short of the glory of God. Jesus did not deal with this woman's sin not one time in this account. She knew she had broken God's law. He did not state the obvious. They knew that according to the law she should be punished. However, Jesus addressed the callousness, aggression and hatred with which they wanted to mete out judgment on this woman. The question that I ask you is this, would you like someone to take the same defensive posture with you as you take with this population? Would you want someone to mete out judgment void of compassion on the sin that you commit? The very posture that we take in this area are so often found in the list of things that God hates yet without mercy and grace we attack instead of draw. We condemn instead of love. The Word has already judged and condemned, we are the hope we are the light we are the way out. That is why I believe Jesus had to deal openly with the religious leaders at this time. There are other reason, I just want to stay on topic here.

B.  Grace says, yes what you did is wrong. Yes what you did deserves punishment even death. Yes you are condemned but that is not what I am going to do. Grace offers you are way out. Grace gives you the opportunity to live in a covenant relationship with Jesus Christ. One could argue that the reason that this woman's heart turned toward Christ is BECAUSE of grace. Because out of every religious leader in the account he was the only one who acted out of and with love. A love that said you are free to confess, renounce, be healed, be delivered, be set from this an walk in newness of life.

As you journey through this training. As you encounter the GLBTQ community you literally find yourself in this same situation. The law will meet grace face to face. The question is which side will you be on…The Law…or Grace?

It is challenging to stay neutral and informative, open and welcoming yet that is exactly what the Lord has required by example from us. Even in practice it is hard to maintain the line of listener, helper and counselor yet the ethical standards of my profession mandate it to be so. It is amazing how many people are able to show compassion and understanding in every other area of this book but will have a very hard time with this particular section. So in understanding how to help compassionately you will also be asked to look inside of yourself, look at your fears and biases that help to fuel the fire of emotionality and hatred that is in your community and congregation as well as see if you are a stumbling block or stepping stone to restoration, and reconciliation.  James 2:9- 13 says it so eloquently, "But if ye have respect to persons, ye commit sin, and are convinced of the law as transgressors.  For whosoever shall keep the whole law, and yet offend in one point, he is guilty of all. _For he that said, Do not commit adultery, said also, Do not kill. Now if thou commit no adultery, yet if thou kill, thou art become a transgressor of the law._ So speak ye, and so do, as they that shall be judged by the law of liberty. For he shall have judgment without mercy, that hath shewed no mercy; and mercy rejoiceth against judgment.

The best place to start is with gaining a clear understanding of what we are speaking of with the acronym GLBTQ community. The simple surface answer is this: Gay, Lesbian, Bisexual,

Transgendered and Questioning. This does no justice to what it is that you are looking at in your communities and congregations. For this reason we are going to review each. You may be wondering why we need to do so. Can't we just pray for them, shove some scripture coupled with a good fire and brimstone message down their throats and move on. No we cannot. Let's do a quick exercise right here, right now to demonstrate. First, look at your key ring. How many of those keys open your front door? How many keys start the ignition of your vehicle? Is it the same key that you used to unlock the door to your home? Exactly. Each door is specific and each key has a specific function For this special population you cannot use a one scripture/sermon fits all technique. How can you skillfully help what you do not understand? Let's begin.

Definitions:

1. Gay. This refers to a man whose sexual preference is toward other men.
2. Lesbian. This refers to a woman whose sexual preference is toward other women
3. Bisexual. This refers to a person who enjoys sexual intimacy with both men and women.
4. Transgendered. This refers to a person who believes that they were born the opposite gender of their sex organs and that their inside does not match their outside. They have taken the steps to correct this.
5. Questioning. This refers to someone who is questioning their sexual identity. They are trying to figure out if they are gay/lesbian, bisexual, or transgendered (Gender Dysphoria).

Just what is it that makes us feel the way that we feel when it comes to this topic? One would speculate that this in and of itself is clean research for the social scientists to study. Perhaps it lies in the unspoken fears that we share. None of what you are about to read is meant to be flip or disrespectful, however, needs to be said. We have got to come out of the closet so to speak with where we are before we can compassionately help this population, who, in their current state, may not feel because of society that they need help.

*Fact.* You cannot catch gay/lesbian. This is not an airborne or commutable disease. This is a lifestyle choice. Just because you are civil to, sit next to or acknowledge this person does not mean you will wake up one day and be gay/lesbian.

*Fact.* Just because that man or woman in your community or congregation likes men or women does not mean that they are attracted to you. There is a fear in the faith based community that all gay / lesbian bisexual persons are they sex crazed deviants who are going to pounce on every person of the same gender that they are. (Yes I put it out there, we have acknowledged the elephant in the living room). The truth is just as you have a personal preference so does the gay/lesbian. In the words of a former patient, "Don't flatter yourself hun, you are not my type."

*Fact.* Just because someone is questioning their sexual orientation does not mean that they have decided to become gay/lesbian/bisexual. It means exactly what it says. They are questioning. This is not the time to shun them or push them away.

*Fact.* There is a difference between and transgendered person and a transvestite. The former is an incongruence in one's birth gender and identified or experienced gender while the latter is a sexual deviancy in which one's cross-dressing behavior generate sexual excitement. (DSM)

*Fact.* Transgendered persons are not deviants who prey on the innocents of society. Neither are transvestites for that matter. However, you will find gender dysphoria in the Diagnostic and Statistical Manual or Psychological Disorders Fifth Edition (DSM -V, APA 2013)


Now that we have learned the differences in this population it is important to understand that there is a story behind each lifestyle choice. You may not want to hear the story but the story is important to them making the choice to come out of this lifestyle choice. It will take patience on your part to learn the story. I spoke with a young man once who was filing a complaint against his physician. I was curious. I understood why I was at Patient Advocacy and I was simply curious as to why this young man was there. (It turned out to be a God thing but that is for a different book) He said to me, "This man said to me, "I'm not interested in why you feel what you feel I just want to treat what you feel' doesn't he realize that the "why" I feel what I feel is just as important to my healing as the "what" I feel? No he just wants to give me drugs and send me away without helping me. I don't need him for my doctor" I shared this to help you in helping this population in you congregations and communities. You cannot help them heal if you do not know what you are helping them to heal from. As stated before this is not a one scripture fits all population and this spirit is a very strong spirit once it has captured someone.

This listening, which is the most powerful thing that we can do with each population in this book, is also the most challenging thing that you will be called upon to do in ministering to them. In the well documented history of Pastor Donnie McClurkin he had been molested several times by make family members in his formidable years. By the time that he hit puberty he thought that this was appropriate that it was right that it was how he was supposed to be. An encounter with Jesus Christ changed his inner man but it took Marvin and Pop Winans as humans to help him to change his outer man. He had to learn how to be a man and to be with a woman.  In the well documented history of Tyler Perry he had been molested by a family member and then when seeking refuge at a friend's home the mother molested him again, leaving him with intimacy issues concerning women. It was not that he didn't not desire a woman, he needed to be healed on the inside from what had happened to trap him into this lifestyle choice. Someone at that pivotal time in their life being date raped may long for the comfort and closeness of someone but having trust issues confuse friendship of the same gender with appropriate love that exists between a man and a woman as is the story of a young woman who asked to remain anonymous. You will not know how to help, if you do not know what you are helping.

When someone is dealing with gender dysphoria (confusion) rules and social norms will not help. What you need to understand and in understanding you cannot help but to be moved with compassion, not disgust, is that this person is living a life in conflict with what he/she sees in the mirror every day. Some of this is created in delivery rooms when a child is born a hermaphrodite and a doctor decides to assign a gender to a child and later the child inside is not what he /she was turned into on the outside. In other delivery room a child was born hermaphroditic and the parent desired a specific gender and requested that it be so. Again we have an issue growing up.

Then living in a society that feels that children should be able to decide for themselves what gender they are has opened many a child up to mass confusion. Society has decided that if a girl is a "tomboy" "is good at sports" " Likes to dress in attire that we have designated "male" or a boy is "compassionate" and "scholarly" "enjoys cooking" whatever then he or she , must have an incongruence with their assigned and identified gender. As a parent, you do not trust the three year old to make correct food choices so why would you allow the same child to make gender choices? In our efforts to "help them be true to themselves" we are failing as parents and mentors to help them to understand that one is a preference and the other is a reality. He/ She was born this gender. Period. This is a struggle every day. In every way. And it is painful and scary because it must be kept a secret or unmercifully judged.

This is a challenging leap for many of you reading this right know, I know, I've been there, but follow me for just one second. Have you ever in your lifetime felt one way on the inside but had to present a totally different way on the outside? Maybe you are very, very shy. Shy to the point that it causes panic attacks to speak in front of a group of people and yet you have a job in which day after day you must speak in front of groups of people. You do a stellar job. Little does anyone know the struggle it took for you to stand up and present, the anxiety that you suffered through to present that lesson or workshop. Perhaps you are very outgoing and exuberant. You love the spotlight and the attention and you are a natural born leader. However, you find yourself is a support position. Maybe you are the Pastor's wife, or the vice president or assistant to the leader. Whatever the case may be, you are called on time after time to not outshine your leader, to let them be all that they are and to push them to their destiny. Of course you can do it, say it, teach it, be it better. But that is not your job. Your job is to sanctify the leader in the eyes of the people. That is hard for you to do day in and day out. Well…that is exactly what is going on with the person in your church or congregation that is struggling with their gender Identity. There is an incongruence between what is on the inside and the outside. They already know it. They live with it every day. They do not need for you to state the obvious. They need for you to guide, listen, support and love. The Lord will do the rest. Don't be a cowboy and drive him or her, become an under-shepherd and lead them to the throne of God.

I want to share this piece of information with you concerning the one you are seeking to minister to who is struggling with Gender Dysphoria or is Transgendered. You must be careful to make sure that what you are dealing with isn't simply what the DSM V calls "Noncomformity to gender roles" For the one with whom you are working with may simply refuse to adhere to stereotypical gender role behavior. There are simply some girls who are more comfortable in everything male. They don't want the make-up, weave, girdle or heels. They love the freedom of the boxers, high-top sneakers and jerseys. There are simply some boys who are comfortable in the kitchen, don't mind showing emotions, are very good at doing hair and sewing garments and are comfortable doing so. They would rather do that then play football or watching boxing. They are not transvestic. There is no sexual gratification associated with those feelings. They are not gender dysphoric, there is no incongruence concerning them. They are just comfortable in their own skin with their own choices and wish to be left alone. This is someone who with modeling and mentorship along with prayer and fasting will learn to at least in public carry themselves in ways that will not cause us who know no better to point, stare and judge.

Finally let's talk briefly about the "Questioning" Population. Take a deep breath. They are questioning. They have not made a decision to be gay/lesbian/bisexual. They have not reached a conclusion that they are living in the wrong body. They have some questions. This is the prime opportunity to teach in love and help guide the decision making process. So many times when a child asks a question parents knee jerk reaction puts up an immediate wall and communication is halted. Hold your breath and listen. This person trusts you. They are telling you that they are questioning their sexuality. This is the time to snatch them as it were from the fire and not push them to it. About ten or twelve years ago when one of my sons were in high school the science teacher challenged each of the boys to have at least one homosexual encounter. He stated, "How do you know that you are not homosexual or at least bisexual if you have never tried it?" This is the type of thing that children are facing today. This is the type of thing that young adults are facing today. By the time my daughter reached high school the gay/straight alliance was in full force and the teacher was happy to "Out" anyone who was questioning. This is not how we are to handle this in the house of God. We have to present the other side of the coin. The side that lets our questioning know that they are fearfully and wonderfully made and that the Lord created for them each an opposite from him /herself to join together with. Don't automatically assume that they are gay/lesbian. Understand that a question is a searching for an answer to help in the decision making process. Let us be wise as serpents yet harmless as doves when we are faced with someone in our midst who is questioning.

## Children of Same Gender Parents

An analysis of fifteen studies involving 500 same-sex parents by Tufts-New England Medical Center in Boston concluded that children from same-sex parents do just as well as children from heterosexual couples. All of these studies very consistently showed that factors such as self-esteem, relationship with peers, intelligence, behavior, and gender identity were the same whether children were raised by heterosexual couples or by same-sex couples.

One study followed children raised by same-sex parents for 11 years as they became adults. The conclusion was still the same: that these adults fared just as well as adults that had been raised by heterosexual parents. Factors analyzed were: sexual orientation identification, self-esteem, relationships with family, the ability to adjust, and underlying psychological issues.

Furthermore, it has been found that the sexual orientation of the parents does not determine what type of parental abilities the parents have. For example, in a study with lesbian couples, it was found that parental abilities and styles were the same between same-sex parents and heterosexual parents - other than the fact that the lesbian couples were more inclined to share household duties and do child rearing on a more equal basis.

There are actually several thousand studies from all types of institutions religious and secular that you can research to see the exact same findings. There are a couple of findings that suggest in the areas of manners, social propriety, acceptance and tolerance children of same sex couple do better than children with heterosexual parents. While it is obvious why these children would fare better in the tolerance and acceptance areas, there is no reason why any child should not have manners and appropriate behaviors. There are also quite a few studies that show children of same sex parents do a little better academically, however, there were other contributing factors that needed to be addressed in those studies. These things speak to bad parenting regardless of one's sexual orientation.

If you have created a safe environment for persons in the GLBTQ community then it is likely that you will run across children of said persons. These children are no different than any other child. Do not treat them as such. Do not tolerate bullying, name calling, disrespect, you know, none of the things that you would tolerate to happen to a special needs child or a child whose parents are going through a divorce. When you become aware of this become a safe place for this child, and advocate and whatever you do, don't cheapen what they are going through by blaming it on their parents.

Before getting to the Do's and Don't's I want to go on record as saying that I am not in one way condoning this sin, nor do I condone any sin. As a social scientist I understand the very fine line that is being walked at the moment not to offend. Many of you may or may not be familiar with the GENOME PROJECT. Is was the largest study of the human body ever conducted. They were looking for genetic causations for a plethora of things one of which is the proff the homosexuality is genetic. Not to anger their sponsors and the popular agenda of society this is what they had to say *"We now know that it is not scientifically accurate to refer to a "gay gene" as the causative agent in homosexuality. The available evidence clearly establishes that no such gene has been identified. Additionally, evidence exists which documents that homosexuals can change their sexual orientation. Future decisions regarding policies about, and/or treatment of, homosexuals should reflect this knowledge."* Statistically speaking neither of these populations in this chapter are as pervasive to society as we are being led to believe. The truth of the matter is that in order to present this population accurately listen to what was stated in research 2013. "If we were making a TV show that honestly reflected homosexuality in America we would need to cast 199 heterosexual actors before casting our first homosexual character." However it is the agenda of today's society to push this lifestyle on everyone and it is up to us to love enough, without throwing stones, to win back to Christ and correct this behavior.

One may say that this is not a spiritual issue but this is exactly what it is. It is a spiritual issue played out on the political arena and we have brothers and sisters being lost because we cannot get past our biases and fears and hatred enough to help. If I were to sum up my personal feelings on this it would have to be by using a quote that I read somewhere that said, "The reason why most people do not come to church is not because of the Gospel. It is because of the unacceptable behavior that is being displayed by the people in the church who say that they speak for the Lord" Rude is rude every day. Mean is mean every day. Just because you are not in agreement with this particular sin does not give us the right or permission to be either for neither is reflective of our compassionate Lord.

## *Things you can do*

- Listen: This is one of the biggest ways to build a trusting relationship in which they will be able to receive your compassion.
- Speak the truth in love. Do not be critical or criticizing of the person. Remember that Sin is sin and just because this person sins differently then you did doesn't make theirs worse.
- Invite and include them. Many times it is not the Gospel that runs this population away. It is the loneliness and ostracization that they receive in the house of God from the people of God. If the church is having a dinner, make it a point to ask them to stay. Step out of your comfort zone and have them sit with you. If the church is having a picnic, invite him or her to the picnic. If you are a Sunday School Teacher, reach out to him or her and make the class safe for him or her.
- Advocate for tolerance of this person, not their sin, but the person. Remember you are not your behavior.
- Love them. Don't talk about love. Show love. Jesus loves them. God is waiting to be reconciled to them. The Holy Spirit is drawing them. So love them. They already have a perverted opinion of love. Show them the real love of Christ manifested through you.

## Things *NOT* to do:

- Don't take a text and start preaching to them. Sinners already know that they are in conflict with God's word. They came to church looking for *a way out* not to be *pointed out.*
- Don't make every conversation that you have filled with anti-GLBTQ scriptures and

condemnation. In fact don't make every conversation about their relationships and preferences period. There is more to the scripture than that. Besides, are you inviting everyone in church into your personal relationships in every conversation? Is there more to you than who you love and who you live with?

- Don't push them into the corner as leave them without a hope. They came to you because of Hope. We believe in the Blessed Hope. The Lord has begotten us again unto a Lively Hope. We are not as those who have NO HOPE, therefore, do not take hope away from him / her.

- Do not SHAME him or her. Jesus took their guilt and stain to the cross. Who are you to shame them? You job is to love them into a saving relationship with the Lord. Then get out of the way and let the Holy Ghost do the rest.

### *LOVE YOUR MEMBER TO LIFE!!!!!*

# ~ PASTOR'S CHILDREN <P K'S> ~

*"Therefore all things whatsoever ye would that men should do to you, do ye even so to them…" Matthew 7:12*

We have all heard the terms: "Life in the fishbowl," and "Living in a glass house." The former is the most accurate description of a Pastor's Child that I know. At least in a house there is wiggle room, room to move around. While everyone is looking at you and watching you there are other rooms in the house or areas of your life that you can meander to. For the Pastor's child there is no escape route. There is only this small confining bowl not allowing room for growth and a constant invasion into the life. Listen to what a couple of Pastor's children have to say about being Pastor's children. There are hundreds of like comments, however these two seem to sum up the majority of what you will find.

At a young age, I was acutely aware of the eternal. I practiced my evangelistic skills on my little sister and my neighborhood friend two houses down. No doubt impacted by my dad's and grandpa's passion for sharing the love of Jesus, my heart was eager to follow their example. As the years passed and my dad became a full-time pastor, my attitude changed. Dad's responsibilities seemed never-ending. Beyond weekly services and premarital counselling, he accommodated demanding personalities and answered constant needs at all hours. Phone calls at 2 a.m., Saturday morning funerals and impromptu counselling sessions became the norm. As a child, all I knew was that it meant less time for me. By the time I reached my late teens, I hated being a pastor's daughter – not simply because I had to share my dad with so many others, but also because of well-meaning church members who placed unrealistic expectations on me as a pastor's kid (PK). People seemed to forget that I was just a teen. I hadn't signed up for nursery duty every week, and I didn't appreciate sideways glances if my sisters and I weren't firmly planted in a pew every time the church doors opened. My passion waned; a subtle, growing resentment moved into my heart."

"Having a pastor for a dad has been a nightmare for many kids. Sadly, many pastors are careful preachers, but crappy dads. Sometimes, it is not the pastor-dad's fault, but an overbearing, unhelpful, and hurtful congregation."

Recent stats from Barna Group research on Pastor's Children says that:

- 40 percent have gone through a period where they significantly questioned their faith
- 33 percent are no longer active in church
- 7 percent no longer consider themselves a Christian

What causes this? Pastors who were asked answered:

- Unrealistic expectations were placed on them (28 percent)
- Negative experiences in church (18 percent)
- Father or mother were too busy at church to spend time with them (17 percent)
- Faith not modeled at home (14 percent)
- Influence of friends or peers (9 percent)

There is so much research out there that one can find to see that we have got to do something to minister to this very special and forgotten population in our churches. On the one hand, I feel badly for the opening of wounds that this particular chapter has caused. On the other hand, I am grateful for the forum it allowed for many of the PKs to express themselves.

It was the response to a blog post I read in June of 2013, speaking on behalf of pastors for their kids, the author summarized seven major things pastors wanted you to know about their children. The article had a big response when it was first posted. But, for reasons I have not completely fathomed, there were almost 200,000 views and hundreds of comments not from pastors but pastor's kids. Being a Social Scientist (Psychologist) I could not let these comments go unnoticed. There was something that society needed to learn from this special population and as any psychologist knows every valid research can be replicated. That follows is what resulted from really looking into this. I think that you will be surprised.

The majority of those who responded were pastors' kids. So, we heard directly from the children themselves. Some were teenagers still living with their parents. Others were adults who grew up as PKs. All of them had pretty strong opinions. As I read again through the plethora of comments, I developed seven major themes from these PKs. Not all of their comments were negative, but a majority did communicate some level of pain. Here is what they said:

1. **The glass house is a reality.** People are always looking at the PKs. They have trouble saying or doing anything without someone, usually a church member, making a comment. Most of these PKs (and former PKs) felt a great deal of discomfort living in the glass house. Some even expressed bitterness.
2. **Some church members made a positive and lasting impression on PKs.** One of the more frequent positive comments we heard were about the church members who loved and cared for the PKs. Many of them took the children under the wings and made a positive difference in their lives.
3. **Some church members were jerks to the PKs.** Many of the stories are heartbreaking. It is really hard to imagine some of the awful words that were said to the PKs. Some still feel the sting of those words decades later.

4. **Many PKs resent the interrupted meals and vacations.** They felt like their pastor parent put the church before the family. One PK, now an adult, lamented that every vacation his family took was interrupted; and many times the vacation was truncated.

5. **Some of the PKs have very positive memories when their parents included them in the ministry.** I read comments about hospital visits, nursing home visits, and ministry in the community. These PKs absolutely loved doing ministry with mom and dad. They felt like the church ministry was something the whole family did.

6. **A key cry from the PKs was: "Let me be a regular kid."** A number of the PKs expressed pain from the high expectations placed upon them by both their parents and church members. Others said that some church members expected them to behave badly because that's just what PKs do.

7. **Some PKs left the church for good because of their negative experiences.** They viewed local congregations as a place for judgmental Christians who are the worst of hypocrites. They have no desire ever to return. You can feel the resentment and pain in their comments. Their hurt is palpable.

Whether you know it or not being a PK is a very stressful position to find oneself in. It is not a role chosen for oneself and it is very difficult to find your own path. PK's are often called upon to do what no other children in the church are called on to do namely: miss out on afterschool activities because they conflict with church service times, have their behavior under constant scrutiny and criticism without much regard for their need of affirmation, expected to be very spiritual and not drawn to the sparkle of the world and the list goes on. They are expected to automatically know how to pray because of who their father is. They are expected to volunteer for every aspect of work in the church gladly and without consideration of their personal time simply because of who their father is. They are expected to listen to constant criticism of not only their parents but themselves without emotion, and the list goes on. Now I ask you, which one of you reading this would allow this to be done to your child? Yet you do it to the Pastor's child.

Life in the PKs fishbowl is tough. Expectations are high. Some people in our congregations may have a habit of forgetting that all children are born in sin, including the preacher's kids. Many congregation members absolve their guilt about their children's behavior by pointing out the flaws they see in PKs. It would do us all well to be aware that the PK is in many ways on trial, not only among church members but in the community as well. We need to remind our congregations that PKs are human-subject to sin and in need of God's grace-is one way to help thwart this problem. We must never fall into the trap of requiring PKs to live up to other people's expectations. However, we all are called to try to live up to God's expectations, but none of us fully succeed.

Abandonment issues are real in the PK population. Abandonment of children does not just happen in homes when a parent physically moves out and ceases to have contact with his or her children. PKs can feel abandoned when we fill up our Pastor's life with so many thing that they are out of sync. When you eat up all of your pastor's time you are forcing him to in action say to his children "You do not matter to as much as everything else in the world (church)," you force his words of love and care of his children to become hollow and meaningless. Being there means not only being physically there, but having their eyes, their affection, and their interest there too. We must be compassionate enough to occasionally allow the Pastor to kick up his heels and have a good time with his children.

PKs of ministry parents who pastor small churches with few children in the church can also feel isolated. Sometimes PKs feel isolated socially as well. Not attending or participating in certain social activities because of ministry demands make PKs feel isolated. If our convictions restrict our children's social activities, we shouldn't just say "No, because we told you so." Rather, we should discuss with them the reasons behind our decisions. Then when they feel isolated, we can offer options for them or at least empathize with them.

## Preachers' Kids
by
Denise Campbell

They're often given a bad name
With people saying they're the worst kind,
And many have been known
To earn the reputation they've been assigned.
It seems that preachers' kids are expected
To live above other kids' level,
And too often people just assume
That preachers' kids are of the devil.
But all Christians should raise their children
To be different from the world's crowd.
If all Christians did their part,
Preachers' kids wouldn't be so singled out.
A child of a preacher has high standards
Expected of them to meet,
But they shouldn't be the only ones,
We all should follow Jesus' feet.
Lord, bless the children whose parents preach,
Help them deny the world and follow You;
And help all Christians raise their kids
To live up to Your holy standards too.
The children of today are the future
And the world has no morals on how to live.
So to teach our kids the Bible way
Is the best thing we can give.
Preachers' kids have a lot to live up to
To be a light out in the world today,
But they are certainly not alone,
We're all expected to live God's way.

## What can I DO?

- **Love them.** They are just like the other kids in your ministry. They want to know you care about them, not because of who their father is, but because of who they are as an individual.
- **Let them be kids.** They are not perfect. They are going to misbehave at times and make mistakes. Don't say, "You should know better. You are the pastor's kid!" This places unrealistic expectations on them.
- **Pour into their lives.** Just because their father is the pastor, that doesn't mean they don't need other people to teach them, mentor them and speak into their lives. Yes, most pastoral parents are their children's primary spiritual influence, but there also needs to be lots of godly leaders who pour into their lives. Like it not you can and will have a part in their decision to follow Christ.

## What should I NOT DO ?

- **Don't mistreat their parents.** When you talk about the pastor or cause strife in the church, you not only bring hurt to him, but you hurt his kids as well. Even if they don't know the details (hopefully their parents are protecting them from the negative side of church), they sense when there is strife and division in the church.
- **Don't place unrealistic expectations on their father that causes him to be gone from home all the time.** Help protect their father's time. They need a father at home just like other kids. Don't contribute to them resenting the church because it took their father away all the time.
- ***Don't Require from Pastor's Child what you are not willing to require from YOURS!!!***

# ~ MEMBERS WHO HAVE CHILDREN WITH DISABILITIES ~

*But Jesus said, Suffer little children, and **forbid them not**, to come unto me: for of such is the kingdom of heaven. Matthew 19:14*

… church can be an unfriendly place. We actually changed churches about 2 years ago
   because  the church we were going to was not at all understanding. At the time,
Teal'c enjoyed being in church. The loud music always made him happy. The people in
the nursery didn't want him in there because they were afraid of him. (he has a feeding
tube, can't talk, they don't know how to care for him ect) so I kept him in service with
me. He was noisy, he'd yell or make excited noises during the music. When the music
was over he's not like a "regular" kid that you can just tell "be quiet" he would make
his happy  noises sometimes during service as well. People started to complain so I
started bringing a stroller and walking around the hallways to keep him quiet. (Missing
the whole service) sometimes I'd stand in the kitchen with him and the baby (Bretac)
in the stroller so the noise didn't filter thru to the main room. Then the tipping point
was when I was in the hallway area with Teal'c and he was making noise. The pastor
told me, in front of everyone, that Teal'c was too distracting and I needed to take him
elsewhere or just not bring him. That was crushing to me, and so I stayed home for
several months until Teyla was born. The pastor's wife had come over to see her and
asked why I hadn't been at church. I told her I felt that there was no point in me going
to be banished to the hallways and miss the whole service anyway because Teal'c was
often noisy. So….she thanked me for "thinking of others" and not coming. Several
people from the church told me I was being selfish expecting others to "deal with" his
noise.  A friend invited me to the church we go to now. They had no issues with
Teal'c's noise and for a while things were great (til the poop thing). The Church is very
understanding of Teal'c's needs and they help me carry him up and down the
stairs….but Teal'c has become so disruptive during service  I've resigned myself to
staying downstairs with him. It's not all bad, because that's where the kid's church is
held too. so I'm there with all my kids for most of service and they still learn a lot. I
really like their kid's program. But it's very hard to deal with the poop thing. That's
something I really can't expect anyone to not be shocked by and the church hasn't
made an issue with it but I did talk to the pastor's wife about it. They said it's no
problem for them if it happens it happens but I'm too embarrassed by it to have it
happen in public again ~Sonya

Sonya & Teal'c

As I read this email, I went through a plethora of emotions. I closed the email without responding. I cried. I prayed. I was angry and didn't understand why. My heart hurt. That was it. I was hurt. I re-read this email. I cried. I prayed. I understood that I needed to pray for this family but I began to pray for the church, for the people who had missed the opportunity to live the scripture that they preach week after week, the scripture that they hide behind justifying themselves as somehow better than others because they are whole. I prayed for my anger. I cried and I cried.

I read this email in its entirety to the ministerial staff at my church. They went through so many emotions during that hour. One began walking the floor, one shook his head, one's eyes filled with tears, and these were the men; one got up and walked into the ladies room and the tears flew, the other sat staring as if in unbelief (these were the women) we were in total disbelief. Comments were made such as "When did the church turn into this?" "So she is not supposed to be able to worship with believers because she has a special needs child? Come on man, who else is supposed to love on that family than the church?" I remembered my husband not to many years ago comforting a mother from the pulpit in the middle of his sermon. The child was a little loud. Without missing a beat he said, "It's okay Sis. The day I can't preach over a child is the day I need to sit down." I remembered the tears that slid down her cheeks in being accepted and loved with her special needs child, who was a runner as well. I remembered the members letting him sit with them so she could have a break, I remember crayons and toys coming out of purses whose children were past that age. I remember the men running more than a few Sundays to keep him from getting out of the door. I thought that we were just like everyone else. *It never entered my mind that this attitude could reside in the house of the Lord.* I cried and I prayed.

I went to work and looked into a student's face with a special needs child and I cried. I looked into the face of Stu and heard the indictment on the church and I got angry...angry because for once he was correct. Not because of this one email but because of the several emails that I received in preparation for this book. I was angry because of conversations I had at different conferences and "religious" settings where hurting mothers expressed these same sentiments. I was moved with compassion. So much so that I fought to make sure that this chapter as personal as I will write it, was included in this book.

Jesus said, "Suffer (Let) the children to come unto me and forbid them not for of such is the kingdom of heaven." Notice he did not say let the healthy children, the easily entreated children, the well behaved children, the pretty children...He said children...ALL CHILDREN. In fact, he rebuked his disciples for trying to keep these mother's with their children away from him. Mark 10:13 says. "But when Jesus saw it, he was much displeased," Let's put it in context Mark 10:13-15 reads, "And they brought young children to him, that he should touch them: and his disciples rebuked those that brought them. But when Jesus saw it, he was much displeased, and said unto them, Suffer the little children to come unto me, and forbid them not: for of such is the kingdom of God. Verily I say unto you, Whosoever shall not receive the kingdom of God as a little child, he shall not enter therein." Let's spend a few pages learning how to help the people in our churches and communities who have children with disabilities.

Isn't every kid special? I think so. But what do we mean when we say "kids with special needs"? This means any kid who might need extra help because of a medical, emotional, or learning problem. These kids have special needs because they might need medicine, therapy, or extra help in school — stuff other kids don't typically need or only need once in a while.

Most parents are familiar with the stresses of child rearing, but there is a special set of tribulations known only to parents of children with disabilities.

A 2009 study by researchers at the University of Wisconsin–Madison found that the physiological and psychological toll on mothers raising autistic children is significantly greater than that on mothers of children who with no disabilities, and that the chronic stress experienced by mothers of autistic children is similar to that of combat soldiers.

Parents of children with disabilities, for example, face a host of questions that most parents never have to address: Should I set up a special needs trust? How can I help my son or daughter navigate the confusing world of dating? Will my daughter ever be able to live on her own?

On learning that their child has a disability, most parents react in ways that are shared by all parents before them who have also been faced with this disappointment and this enormous challenge. One of the first reactions is *denial*—"This cannot be happening to me, to my child, to our family." Denial rapidly merges with *anger*, which may be directed toward the medical personnel who were involved in providing the information about the child's problem. Anger can also color communication between husband and wife or with grandparents or significant others in the family. Early on, it seems that the anger is so intense that it touches almost anyone, because it is triggered by the feelings of *grief* and inexplicable *loss* that one does not know how to explain or deal with.

*Fear* is another immediate response. People often fear the unknown more than they fear the known. Having the complete diagnosis and some knowledge of the child's future prospects can be easier than uncertainty. In either case, however, fear of the future is a common emotion: "What is going to happen to this child when he is five years old, when he is twelve, when he is twenty-one? What is going to happen to this child when I am gone?" Then other questions arise: "Will he ever learn? Will he ever go to college? Will he or she have the capability of loving and living and laughing and doing all the things that we had planned?" Other unknowns also inspire fear. Parents fear that the child's condition will be the very worst it possibly could be. Memories return of persons with disabilities one has known. Sometimes there is guilt over some slight committed years before toward a person with a disability. There is also fear of _society's rejection_, fears about how brothers and sisters will be affected, questions as to whether there will be any more brothers or sisters in this family, and concerns about whether the husband or wife will love this child. These fears can almost immobilize some parents.

Then there is *guilt*—guilt and concern about whether the parents themselves have caused the problem: "Did I do something to cause this? Am I being punished for something I have done? Did I take care of myself when I was pregnant? Did my wife take good enough care of herself when she was pregnant?" Much self-reproach and remorse can stem from questioning the causes of the disability.

Guilt feelings may also be manifested in spiritual and religious interpretations of blame and punishment. When they cry, "Why me?" or "Why my child?" many parents are also saying, "Why has God done this to me?" How often have we raised our eyes to heaven and asked: "What did I ever do to deserve this?" One young mother said, "I feel so guilty because all my life I had never had a hardship and now God has decided to give me a hardship."

*Confusion* also marks this traumatic period. As a result of not fully understanding what is happening and what will happen, confusion reveals itself in sleeplessness, inability to make decisions, and mental overload. In the midst of such trauma, information can seem garbled and distorted. You hear new words that you never heard before, terms that describe something that you cannot understand. You want to find out what it is all about, yet it seems that you cannot make sense of all the information you are receiving. Often parents are just not on the same wavelength as the person who is trying to communicate with them about their child's disability.

**Powerlessness** to change what is happening is very difficult to accept. You cannot change the fact that your child has a disability, yet parents want to feel competent and capable of handling their own life situations. It is extremely hard to be forced to rely on the judgments, opinions, and recommendations of others. Compounding the problem is that these others are often strangers with whom no bond of trust has yet been established.

**Disappointment** that a child is not perfect poses a threat to many parents' egos and a challenge to their value system. This jolt to previous expectations can create reluctance to accept one's child as a valuable, developing person.

**Rejection** is another reaction that parents experience. Rejection can be directed toward the child or toward the medical personnel or toward other family members. One of the more serious forms of rejection, and not that uncommon, is a "death wish" for the child—a feeling that many parents report at their deepest points of depression.

During this period of time when so many different feelings can flood the mind and heart, there is no way to measure how intensely a parent may experience this constellation of emotions. Not all parents go through these stages, but it is important for parents to identify with all of the potentially troublesome feelings that can arise, so that they will know that **they are not alone**.

Something else that is encountered that many overlook is the way in which we speak. Listen to a minute to the words from Sonya,

"What bothers us is when people use medical terms to describe someone who's being "stupid on purpose" or something. (like using the word "retarded" as an insult when it's your kid's actual diagnosis. Yes, that is one of Teal'c's many diagnosis. It doesn't bother me at all that it's a medical description of his brain function but it bothers the heck out of me when I hear people using the "r" word as an insult. It gets under my skin even more when people tell me I'm just being overly sensitive about it. It's like when they say "oh that's so "retarded" when they think something is dumb/ stupid or unfair they are saying "oh that's so like Teal'c" or something like that. I know that's not really what they mean but that's kind of what it says to parents of mentally disabled people.

Wow! Did you see that one coming? I have to be honest, that the research and preparation of this chapter has made me super sensitive to things   like this. Not just sensitive but moved to do or say something. I find that people do not mean to be insensitive, they have just not learned how to be sensitive. One thing that you can you is interrupt someone right in the middle of the conversation and say, "Do you actually know anyone who is retarded?" I do, his/her name is_____. What I just heard you saying when describing this incident is that the person is such a _____. Is that what you meant? How can we say that a little differently? People are taken aback but that is your opportunity to teach. Face it, you don't know what you don't know until you know it. I have found myself saying, "Disabilities come in all forms. Some obviously notable others not. You do not know who in this room is developmentally delayed, retarded or has other special needs. How do you think they and or their family member heard what you just said? I know that you didn't mean to be cruel nor offensive but it is what it is whether it was your intent or not. Let's look at how we can say this differently." Most times the person no longer wants to tell the story, but I've heard them "venting" about what I said to them. It makes me happy because in their anger at me they are educating others. I know because I have heard others respond, "Wow, that's deep, I didn't think about it that way" This is just another way in which you can help or minister to parents who have children with special needs.

I am enclosing a different type of Do's and Don'ts in this section. It is the reply of one of my research persons, whom I have never met but was happy to hear that there are people in the pews who want to know how to do better, how to help. I believe that we can gain so much more through her list than anything that I could come up with. Thank you Adrienne.

Here is a long list of things we parents of kids with mental/emotional/social issues hear often and that hurt us, and a much shorter list of things that I wish I had heard back in the years when life was all crisis, all the time.

Adrienne & Carter

1. **What you said:** God never gives us more than we can handle.
   **What we heard:** You're fine. Quit whining.
   **The reality:** We're not fine. Also, it is very dangerous to bring God into conversation with a person whose faith you don't know intimately (and sometimes even then). We bring God to these conversations by bringing kindness. We bring God by seeing, hearing, and connecting.

2. **What you said:** He seems fine to me! *Or*, All kids do that!
   **What we heard:** You are a very dramatic person and you should get over yourself. Also, you are very likely a huge liar.
   **The reality:** If you said this to me now, I would raise my left eyebrow to you and make a mental note never to discuss anything related to Carter again. Back when I was in agony pretty much all the time, it was like being punched in the guts. It didn't help that I heard it often. Here is a good rule for all of us when we are talking to a person in pain: do not contradict. Acknowledge the pain. See the person in front of you, because the person matters infinitely more than the facts, and this isn't a courtroom. The pain is real.

3. **What you said:** You must be a very special parent for God to give you such a special child.
   **What we heard:** We are fundamentally different. I'm not even going to try to understand you. **The Reality:** I'm not special, and I need you to see and hear me and my struggle.

4. **What you said:** You are an angel! I could never do what you're doing.
   **What we heard:** Hey, sounds tough. What a bummer. It's a good thing you can totally handle it and you don't need anything from me!
   **The Reality:** Yes, I can handle it. The alternative is…what? We handle it. Not with any grace or style, you just do. Ordinary you, ordinary me.

*Note from Adrienne* "We aren't different, we parents of special needs kids. I promise I'm just like you. You'd be horrified if you heard a group of parents of kids with issues like Carter's talking amongst ourselves; we use gallows humor and talk in ways we know would alienate you, and we are very un-angel-like. We are deeply angry sometimes. Wounded. Broken. But if you come to us and say, *hey, I'm in trouble, I have a kid with problems and I think I belong in your club,* we will gather you into our circle so fast you won't quite know what hit you. We will listen to you cry and we won't tell you to stop. We won't tell you to be strong because we know you are being exactly as strong as you can be. We know that your need is deep and that you can't handle this, even as you are in the midst of handling it.

5. ***What you said***: Every child is a blessing.
   ***What we heard***: Suck it up, buttercup!
   ***The Reality***: Of course my child is a blessing. I love him like fire. That does not invalidate my pain. In fact, my love is causing my pain because if I didn't love him, why would I even care?

6. ***What you said***: Your faith will get you through! *Or,* God doesn't bring us to it unless he plans to bring us through it! *Or,* With God all things are possible!
   ***What we heard***: You're only having trouble because your faith is crappy and weak.
   ***The Reality***: Here's the deal: my faith *did* get me through, or rather, God did. I was more broken by the time Carter had his second birthday than I have ever revealed publicly, and I spent long, wakeful nights in the manner that is familiar to millions of people of faith: on my knees, the holy book open in front of me, begging God for relief for me and my family and healing for my child. The presence of God in the universe doesn't let people of faith off the hook and platitudes like this don't help anyone except the person who says them. People who are suffering need something more substantial. If you are a person of faith, we need you to live that faith by caring for us and hearing how we're struggling.

7. ***What you asked***: Did you take medicine while you were pregnant?
   ***What we heard:*** How did you cause this?
   ***The Reality:*** We don't have (will never have) answers to questions like *why this child? Why our family?* There *are* no answers to those questions, or at least none to which we have access during this lifetime.

Here is a map that my support group complied to help you to help us:

**Listen. Just listen**. Open yourself up. Yes, it hurts and it's very scary. That's OK. There is a person in front of you who is in pain. Don't leave her alone with it.

**<u>Know that you can't fix it</u>**. Don't try. We have doctors and therapists and other professionals for treatment.

**<u>Acknowledge and affirm</u>**. Say, *wow that sounds hard.* Say, *oh, my God, how painful!* Say, *I hate that it's so difficult for you.*

**<u>Treat our kids the same way you treat other children in your life</u>**. Of course you should be sensitive, especially with kids who have emotional/social/behavioral issues, because many of them don't want to be touched or may not be verbal, but in general, if you usually engage kids in conversation, do that with our kids too. Say hello. Smile. They might not respond predictably, if they respond at all, but they see you.

**<u>Offer to help, but only if you mean it</u>** (people in pain are sensitive; we know when you're saying words you don't mean so you can feel good about yourself). My mom sometimes came to my house and gathered all my laundry baskets and every scrap of dirty laundry in the house (which completely filled the trunk of her car) and brought it all back a day or two later, clean and folded. Our friends from church occasionally brought us meals. A friend drove Carter and me to some of his appointments during the worst months because I didn't feel safe driving alone with him. Those things meant the world to me. As much as I appreciated the clean clothes, meals, and rides, I was even more grateful to feel a little less alone in the world.

**<u>Send a note, a text, or an email</u>**. Parenting a child with special needs can be profoundly lonely. It's also hectic and chaotic and we may not respond to you, but do it anyway. The world starts to feel very far away when life is all appointments, crisis, chaos, and praying for survival. Stay connected, even if it feels one-sided.

**<u>If you're very close, spend a little time learning about your friend's child's diagnosis</u>**. There is no need to become an expert, but an evening spent learning will only make you a better listener. If you don't know what to read, your friend will gladly tell you.

**<u>Just show up and listen</u>**. There's nothing any person in pain needs more.

# ~ ADDICTIONS & RECOVERY~

*"When Jesus heard it, he saith unto them, They that are whole have no need of the physician, but they that are sick: I came not to call the righteous, but sinners to repentance." Mark 2:17*

## ~ Addiction ~

According to the American Society of Addiction Medicine the **Short Definition of Addiction is as follows:**

Addiction is a primary, chronic disease of brain reward, motivation, memory and related circuitry. Dysfunction in these circuits leads to characteristic biological, psychological, social and spiritual manifestations. This is reflected in an individual pathologically pursuing reward and/or relief by substance use and other behaviors.

Addiction is characterized by inability to consistently abstain, impairment in behavioral control, craving, diminished recognition of significant problems with one's behaviors and interpersonal relationships, and a dysfunctional emotional response. Like other chronic diseases, addiction often involves cycles of relapse and remission. Without treatment or engagement in recovery activities, addiction is progressive and can result in disability or premature death.

As you can see, addiction is not a matter of weak character or lack of willpower. Addiction is a disease.

The Center for Disease Control criteria for classification allows Chemical dependency to be classified as a disease. This disease comes in various forms and manifests itself in a myriad of ways in the house of God. What we need to remember is that everyone who is addicted to anything is not the "stereotypical gutter hugger/street walker" The first thing that we should look at is the criteria for a disease and how addiction fits that criteria.

1. First and foremost a disease must be ***primary*** which means it is not caused by anything else. No one sneezed on you and you caught it. You did not develop it from a cut or a bruise.
2. Next a disease must be ***progressive*** meaning that it gets worse the longer that it is not treated or mistreated. I will go deeper into this a little later.
3. Next a disease is ***pervasive*** which means that it interferes with every area of ones existence as well as those in relationship with them.
4. After meeting the first three criteria diseases are ***chronic*** which means once you have it you always have it. It may go into remission but you still have it.

Have you ever heard the phrase, "Once an alcoholic always an alcoholic?" or "Once a diabetic always a diabetic?"

5. All diseases are **_treatable_**. However, treatment does not equal cure. Treatment equals management.

6. All diseases are potentially **_fatal_**. What prevents early death because of the disease is the management of it.

Loot at the chart below comparing diabetes to addiction to explain this disease concept a little further.

### Chemical Dependency vs. Diabetes

### A Look at Chemical Dependency as a Disease

| DIABETES | CHEMICAL DEPENDENCY |
|---|---|
| 1. Diagnosed by a set of symptoms: Poloyuria (urinate frequently)<br><br>Polyphasia ( always hungry)<br><br>Polydipssia (always thirsty)<br><br>Weak / shaky<br><br>Sweats | 1. Diagnosed by a set of symptoms: Use of MAC<br><br>Denial ( of problem with MAC)<br><br>Problems in family<br><br>Problems in relationships<br><br>Physical problems<br><br>Emotional problems<br><br>Legal problems |
| 2. Progressive illness Will get worse if untreated<br><br>Terminal illness (death) | 2. Progressive illness<br><br>Will get worse if untreated<br><br>Terminal illness (death, prison, psychiatric institutionalization) |

| | |
|---|---|
| 3. Genetic predisposition<br>The more family members with the illness, the more likely that chances that you'll have it too. | 3. Genetic predisposition<br><br>The more family members with the<br><br>illness, the more likely that chances<br><br>that you'll have it too. |
| 4. No cure but it can be controlled | 5. No cure but it can be controlled |
| 6. Control involves active participation of sufferer | 6. Control involves active participation of sufferer |
| 7. Control implies responsibility on the part of the diabetic.<br>Knowledge of the disease<br><br>Knowledge of treatment regime<br><br>Diet<br><br>Medication<br><br>Support groups | 7. Control implies responsibility on the part of the chemically dependent.<br>Knowledge of the disease<br><br>Knowledge of treatment regime<br><br>Abstinence<br><br>AA/NA Support Groups<br><br>Psychotherapy |
| 8. The diabetic I not responsible for having the disease.<br>The diabetic is responsible for controlling it | 8. The chemically dependent is not responsible for having the disease.<br><br>The chemically dependent is<br><br>responsible for controlling it. |
| 9. Diabetes can be caused by an underlying physical disorder:<br>Pancreatitis<br><br>Pancreatic cancer | 9. Chemical dependency can be caused by an underlying emotional<br><br>disorder:<br><br>Depression<br><br>Bipolar disorder<br><br>Personality disorder |

Refer to your workbook in the section of Addictions and Recovery for more information on the Disease concept. What is important to remember, however, is that it doesn't matter what the addiction there needs to be a paradigm shift in our thinking if we are going to help this population. If this person in your congregation had recently been diagnosed with diabetes how would you begin to help them? You would learn about the disease. You would learn about the current stage that it is in and you would make adjustments in everyday living as you helped them to learn how to manage or even reverse so to speak this disease. The same is necessary for the disease of addiction.

"So how can I, an ordinary individual who sits in the pew or on the porch know what I am looking at in terms of a person's addiction?" you may ask. Well, just as diabetes has stages and a different modality or care for each treatment, so does addiction. Let's take a look first at diabetes and then at addiction.

Metabolic Syndrome, Pre Diabetes. The patient is told that they are borderline diabetic. They need to adjust their diet. Get exercise. In some cases lose weight and the disease will go no further.

Stage 1 diabetes. The disease has progressed. You are prescribed a pill like Metformin that you need to take. But no. Now you are ready to change your diet and begin exercising. What your denial has prevented you from understanding is that your disease has progressed to the point that diet and exercise will not manage this disease any more.

Stage 2 diabetes. The disease has progressed further. Now you need insulin shots. You feel that you have received a wakeup call and you are invested in the pills. However, the disease has progressed further than this

Now you experience things like blindness or amputations etc. Because the disease has progressed so far improperly treated. If you do not make drastic life style changes you will die. At any stage following the protocol to manage the disease would have prevents one from reaching this place. So it is with the progression of addiction regardless to what one is addicted to. I like to explain it like this:

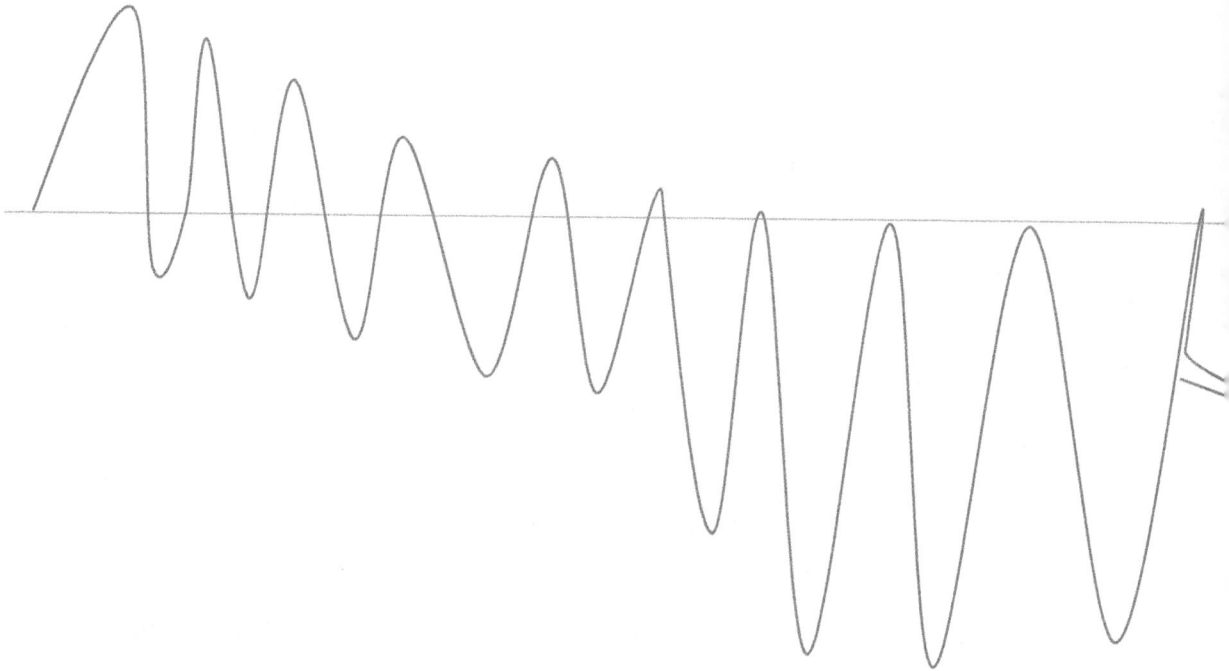

When one begins their journey in Addiction the initial high or euphoria that is experienced is so great that the person is constantly attempting to experience that same feeling again. The truth however is that the initial euphoria is never achieved. What happens is that the highs get lower and the lows get deeper until a person is actually simply using just so that they can feel normal. How can that be you may ask? Well, each person as a specific amount of several chemicals that are supposed to be in their bodies at any given time. When the chemical is introduced from an outside source (alcohol, marijuana, excessive sex, social media, shopping whatever) the brain goes into a type of panic mode. It desperately tries to regulate that chemic. Because it cannot the brain simply stops producing it. Now the person must use or engage simply to get sufficient chemical in the body to function properly. Thus the cycle of addiction.

## Progression of Addiction

Early – euphoria without penalty, without withdrawal, tolerance increasing.

Middle Stage – Withdrawal begins to emerge. Psychological pain emerges, social withdrawal occurs. There are problems but much denial that it is related to addiction.

Chronic – definite physical deterioration (cirrhosis of the liver, GIT ulcers, heart problems, brain affected, family separation, loss of job, STI's, bankruptcy, etc.)

- Short-term gratification
- Long-term pain
- Addictive thinking
- Increased tolerance
- Loss of control
- Bio-psycho-social damage.

What I have just described is a cycle of addiction that leads the addicted person into a deadly trap. Let's take a closer look at this cycle and what happens to when the person that you want to help becomes trapped in it.

**Short-term gratification**: First there is short term gratification. You feel good now. There is a strong short-term gain that causes you to assume that drug or behavior is good for you.

**Long-term pain and dysfunction**: The short-term gratification is eventually followed by long-term pain. This pain, part of which is from physical withdrawal, and part of which is from the inability to cope psycho-socially without drugs, is the direct consequence of using the addictive drugs.

**Addictive Thinking**: The long-term pain and dysfunction trigger addictive thinking. Addictive thinking begins with **obsessions** and **compulsion**. Obsession is a continuous thinking about the positive effects of using alcohol and drugs. Compulsion is an irrational urge or craving to use the drug to get the positive effect even though you know it will hurt you in the long run. This leads to **denial** and **rationalization** in order to allow continued use. Denial is the inability to recognize there is a problem. Rationalization is blaming other situations and people for problems rather than use.

**Increased Tolerance**: Without your being aware that it is happening, more and more of the drug is required to produce the same effect.

**Loss of Control**: The obsession and compulsion become so strong that you cannot think about anything else. Your feelings and emotions become distorted by the compulsion. You become stressed and uncomfortable until finally the urge to use is so strong that you cannot resist it. Once you use the addictive chemicals or the addictive behaviors again, the cycle starts all over again.

**Bio-Psycho-Social Damage:** Eventually there is damage to the health of your body (physical health), and relationships with other people (social health). As pain and stress get worse, the compulsions to use addictive drugs or behaviors to get relief from pain increases. A deadly trap develops. You need addictive use in order to feel good. When you use addictively you damage yourself physically, psychologically and socially. This damage increases your pain which increases your need for addictive use.

Why spend so much time on this? Because depending on where this person that you are called to help lies on the continuum determines how effective you can be in helping. The deeper into this the more physically impossible it is to tangibly help them. Never, however, forget that PRAYER changes. Prayer can move this person to admitting that they are powerless over this addiction and their life has become unamenable. That is when help can start. That is when you can be there. Until then. Pray. Pray. Watch and pray. And addict will steel from his or her mother. They will tell you whatever they feel that you need to hear to gain your trust so that they can take from you. There is not conscious on the need for the addiction. You need to be in the words of our Savior, "As wise as a serpent, yet as gentle as a dove." Never assume because your heart is in the right place and you want to help that the person is wanting to be helped. However, there are some specific things that you can do once the person is ready for your compassionate care.

- Understand that recovery hurts and it is confusing. See you are asking a person to cut of their dominant hand and do everything with the remaining hand. I know that sounds crazy but that is what they have to learn. They have to learn to deal with life on life's terms. Instead of resulting to the tried and true (use, shopping, social media etc) you have to feel it face it and move through it.
- Listen. Everyone needs someone to listen. There is a reason for this addiction. There is a payoff for what is happening. They need help to figure out what the payoff is…the why. Then they need you to listen as they figure out now. Meaning, how I can get this need met, how can I deal with this issue without the addiction.

- Do not pity or ease up because they are pursuing recovery. It is easy to go back if one is not paying attention to the triggers and the cues to using. This is a lifetime, lifestyle disease.

~ Recovery ~

*"... And Jesus said unto her, Neither do I condemn thee: go, and sin no more" John 8:11*

Before out time on recovery I feel that it is important that you understand the difference between abstinence and recovery as well as the concept of cross addiction.

Cross addiction is when a person cannot use the substance that they want to so they develop a dependence on something else. It is easy to understand when you see someone who cannot afford cocaine so they smoke crack, or someone who can not engage in excessive sex or smoke as many cigarettes as they would like so they begin to substitute food specifically caffeine and sugars for sex and nicotine. But there is a more heinous perversion of cross addiction that Satan has coupled with abstinence that is infiltrating the church because we as a church are not educated in the world of addiction. That cross addiction is **CHURCH.**

Yes, we want this fragile person to come to church and we are happy because they are not out engaging in their addiction, however we must watch and pray and discern that this attendance in church is not a cross addiction. You can tell this when you have someone who has ceased using or spending or gambling or eating whatever it is and they become "Super Saint" They are in church every time the door opens and they are not satisfied with the number and times of services. They "NEED" more church and more church and more church. They cannot get enough service. They are attending your services and then every service that they can find when you are not in service at your church. You need to look at this closely.

First, the fact that they need to be in church should cause you some pause. What is happening that they need to be here so much? Are they developing a tolerance for church meaning are they needing more and more service to experience the same results as when they started? Are they chasing some euphoric release? That is not worship. Worship is not a cross addiction. What is the reason that they are showing up to church? Is it for the same reasons that they used in the beginning? That means that the causations of addiction have not been dealt with. Deliverance has not taken place. It is being substituted with church. If this is not dealt with. If deliverance is not achieved this person will eventually return to using because they never entered into recovery and they will not be able to find a ministry to keep up with their increased need.

Let's briefly look at the differences between Abstinence and recovery so that you may ask God more specifically how to help.

- _**Abstinence**_ is when a person is no longer engaging in their addiction because they cannot do so. There is something that is prohibiting the engagement such as jail, divorce whatever the stipulation put on the person that will result in significant loss of freedom or family. This person is not in recovery but is the most challenging person to help. Mostly because they turn into what is termed, "A DRY DRUNK" This term has nothing to do with alcohol. It refers to a person who no longer engages in their addiction, however, that is the only thing that has changed. Their behavior is still the same. Their thought processes are still the same. Their problem solving strategies are still the same. The only thing different about this person is that they no longer engage in the addiction. It is like the person who come to the altar ask the Lord to save them and never becomes a new creature. The old stays and the new never comes. This person believes that he/she is ok because they are not engaging in the addiction. This person may or may not develop a religious cross addiction. This is a person that your best compassionate care is PRAYER.

-

- Recovery is when a person has chosen to live life without the addiction, has son the work of healing and changing their environment etc. This is the sanctification process as it were for this person. This is the time where the teachers and mentors in the congregation or community are important. You have to teach how to do it differently. You have to model how to be appropriate in our responses to life's stressors. You have to love this person to life. This is the new convert personified. Just as you can't expect the new convert to automatically know how to live this Christian life, to know what the Lord requires, you can't expect it from the person in recovery. They need to learn both naturally and spiritually.

According to SAMSHA recovery **is** a process of change through which individuals improve their health and wellness, live a self-directed life, and strive to reach their full potential. Furthermore, SAMHSA has delineated four major dimensions that support a life in recovery:

- _Health_: overcoming or managing one's disease(s) as well as living in a physically and emotionally healthy way;
- _Home:_ a stable and safe place to live;

- **Purpose:** meaningful daily activities, such as a job, school, volunteerism, family caretaking, or creative endeavors, and the independence, income and resources to participate in society; and
- **Community:** relationships and social networks that provide support, friendship, love, and hope.

So how can you help?

Health

- Encourage this person to get a "recovery physical" This is more in-depth than the yearly well person physical. It alerts the PCP that this person has abused drugs, sex or food. They will look for organic damage that would never come up if they were not alerted of the need to look. This will help the person to find out exactly what life changes if any are need on this journey. This is scary.
- Be that person whose is a support to them. Teach them scripture that will bring peace or emotional health. Feed them the WORD as often as you can without being preachy or judgmental.

Home

- The worse thing a person in recovery can do is return to their using environment. This is where you can see the power of being unequally yoked with unbelievers. Help them to find a new place to live if possible. Help them to find a strategy of escape to a safe place if necessary for respite time. What happens plain and simple is that this person's health is forcing their family and friends to see just how unhealthy they are. It is easier to cause this person to return to how they were so that things stay the same than it is to put the personal work in and change. It isn't as if they held a meeting and decided to set this person up. It is subconscious but it is real. Isn't that the same struggle that the new convert has? So without help they will be lured or pulled back into where they just left.
- Help the person to find a new social group. A healthy group of people who are not using buddies, shopping buddies, sex buddies whatever it was. By the time most people enter into recovery they have pushed everyone away and their using buddies are all that they feel they have. You can be a person for them. You can bring them

into your circle. You can mentor and guide to leaning to hear the Holy Spirit who will guide us into change.

## Purpose

- The commentary above is really self-explanatory. However some things that you can do in your church is to help this person discover their place and their giftedness. They may not be able to see past their past enough to see a place for them in the kingdom. Many times they are so happy to have their name in the Lambs book that it doesn't occur to them without support and guidance that there is something else that they can do. We don't testify any more so many times they see our now without a clue of where God brought us from. They need to know. How did Paul say it, "Know ye not that the unrighteous shall not inherit the kingdom of God? Be not deceived: neither fornicators, nor idolaters, nor adulterers, nor effeminate, nor abusers of themselves with mankind, Nor thieves, nor covetous, nor drunkards, nor revilers, nor extortioners, shall inherit the kingdom of God. *And such were some of you: but ye are washed, but ye are sanctified,* **but ye are justified in the name of the Lord Jesus, and by the Spirit of our God**.

- In your community you can point to some of the very things that are talked about. Depending on the Addiction they may not be able to do some things but there are things that can be done. Because of the addiction there are people and things in the neighborhood that they never noticed because it did not serve them in their addiction. Help them to see. A community garden is one thing in a sea of many that will help him / her to feel productive, able to give back, have purpose.

Community: This is what the church is supposed to be all about. Help them to find their place in the community. Show him/her the love of Christ. Help them to B-E-L-O-N-G. That is what all of us need. You have received so much by way of community in the church that maybe until just now you hadn't taken for granted and forgot about. But this is life to the person in recovery. The community has to be strong enough that they help this person resist the pull that is trying to ensnare them once again into bondage.

## ~ Let Go, Let God ~
## ~ Author Unknown ~

To Let Go doesn't mean to stop caring;
it means I can't do it for someone else.

To Let Go is not to cut myself off;
it's the realization that I can't control another.

To Let Go is not to enable,
but to allow learning from natural consequences
To Let Go is to admit powerlessness,
which means the outcome is not in my hands.

To Let Go is not to try to change or blame another;
it's to make the most of myself.

To Let Go is not to care for,
but to care about.

To Let Go is not to fix,
but to be supportive.

To Let Go is not to judge,
but to allow another to be a human being.

To Let Go is not to be in the middle arranging all the outcomes,
but to allow others to affect their own destinies.

To Let Go is not to be protective;
it is to permit another to face reality.

To Let Go is not to deny,
but to accept.

To Let Go is not to nag, scold, or argue,

but instead to search out my own shortcomings and correct them.

To Let Go is not to adjust everything to my desires,
but to take each day as it comes, and to cherish myself in it.

To Let Go is not to regret the past,
but to grow and live for the future. To Let Go is to fear less and to love more.

# ~ ABUSE IN THE HOUSE OF GOD ~

*"In the same day also will I punish all those that leap on the threshold, which fill their masters' houses with violence and deceit" Zephaniah 1:9*

I once saw the following framed card in an office: "On the street I saw a small girl cold and shivering in a thin dress, with little hope of a decent meal. I became angry and said to God: why did you permit this? Why don't you do something about it? For a while God said nothing. That night He replied quite suddenly: I certainly did something about it. — *I made you*."

Edmund Burke once said, "All that is necessary for evil to triumph is that good men (and women) do nothing."

These are sobering thoughts yet I feel they are the most compelling introduction to this chapter. Please remember that with as much information as there is "out there" on abuse of all kinds, this is still the most taboo subject in "churchdom universal". Many times I would say to a patient, "You are only as sick as your secrets" The church is very "sick" because it endeavors to keep this "a secret" as if not talking about it will make it go away, or as if the bible does not address it. The bible most explicitly speaks about it. I also would say to certain patients, "Once it is no longer a secret, it no longer has power over you." There are hurting people in our churches and their voices need to be heard regardless of the abuse that they are experiencing whether it be child abuse, elder abuse, and sexual abuse, the abuse of the disabled or religious abuse (church hurt)

We've all been in situations where something has happened or someone has disclosed something to us and we act as if we don't see it or don't hear it. Jesus tells a story like that, where the religious leaders who should have helped, ignored and walked by someone who was beaten, who was laying on the side of the road (Luke 10:25-37).

Could Jesus have been talking about you? Or me?

Men, women, and children who attend our church and live in our neighborhood are suffering in homes where abuse is present. Yet we don't want to see it, and it's easy to ignore. But that would be wrong. It hurts them, and it hurts us. When we ignore someone desperate for help, they continue to suffer and we lose our humanity.

Jesus tells his followers, "Whenever you helped someone who was overlooked or ignored, that was me–you did it to me." (Matthew 25:40 The Message). When we take our time to help someone, Jesus says that we are ministering to Him.

### The Problem with the Word "Abuse"

It is safe to say that we live in a culture which frequently (and ironically) abuses the word "abuse." One of the most common ways that this has been done has been by incorrectly locating the meaning of the word "abuse" in "the *perception* of mistreatment," rather than mistreatment itself. During the 1980s and into the '90s, the notion that subjective perceptions, rather than objective behavior, determine whether something was "abusive" succeeded in infiltrating academia, the media, and even our judicial system to an astonishing degree.

As a society, we have paid a huge price for this. It has led to some rather ironic and even bizarre developments. The word "abuse" came to be regularly resorted to as both a ready weapon of accusation, and a proven shield of defense in our court systems. Lawyers worked hard to absolve their clients for murders committed on the basis of some childhood "abuse" they experienced, even while therapists persuaded young women that the real reason for their depression was that they were abused in a Satanic ritual as children, or perhaps sexually by their fathers. The "abuse fad" made many people a lot of money while ruining more than a few lives.

It also trivialized the *real* incidents of abuse, and made it less likely that they would be taken seriously in the long run. In any situation where the social pendulum swings too far in one direction, backlash is inevitable, and in this case the backlash was soon underway. The mid-1990s, witnessed scores of media reports telling of the horror of people locked up or otherwise deprived of their rights, sometimes on the flimsiest of so-called "evidence of abuse."

## Domestic Violence

There are three major kinds of abuse within a relationship: Physical abuse when someone hits, slaps, beats, burns, kicks, or stabs you. But it also includes arm grabbing, shaking or being pushed.

There is sexual abuse, which is any exploitation of your body against your will. And there is emotional abuse, which is wide spread and very misunderstood.

Emotional abuse is when someone threatens or humiliates you. This includes name-calling, putting you down, insulting you, or breaking your things. Control is a huge part of emotional abuse and involves chronic anger, jealousy, accusations, and distrust. The main symptoms that you maybe experiencing emotional abuse include feeling depressed, anxious, and unhappy in your relationship, that you feel isolated and that you're down on yourself, or even hate yourself, especially when you're together.

October is Domestic Violence awareness month. Domestic Violence is defined as: violent or aggressive behavior within the home, typically involving the violent abuse of a spouse or partner.

Many people think that the Bible has very little to say about abuse, and yet there are countless bible verses which speak clearly and definitely on the subjects of domestic abuse and domestic violence.

Quite often, if we as victims approach and confide in an elder, priest, or member of our Church, hoping for some support and encouragement, we can leave feeling even guiltier and trapped than we did formerly. We may be told that the abuse is due to our own lack of submissiveness, or our own sinfulness, that we would not suffer if our faith was greater, or that we will be rewarded in the next life for the suffering we experience in this one (!?!). I have heard of women who have been told earnestly by their pastors and members of their church that it would be better for them to die at the hands of their abusive husband than to seek a separation and protection for their children!

When talking to Church members we have to realize that understanding of Domestic Abuse is still in its infant stages in many Churches, and that the majority of people (including its leaders whatever their title) still hold basic misconceptions regarding the dynamics of an abusive relationship and have formed their opinions less on what Scripture says, and more on those myths generally held in society. An added hurdle is to be found especially in the more fundamental denominations, where the mistaken belief is often that such things may happen "in the World", but not in a good Christian home!

**The question, however, for every Christian person should not be what does our Church say about our situation, but what does the LORD say to us in the Bible**, according to which both our Church should be based, and more importantly, according to which we, as individuals, should try to live?

It has not been my norm in this book to flood one with scripture because, as stated in the beginning, the Lord gives us specific scripture unique to us as individuals and those to whom he will be sending us. However, in this chapter I am going to veer away from that and simply state what the bible has to say on various aspect of abuse. I do this because many of us really may not know where to draw from the Word when faced with this member sitting next to us during morning worship or on the porch across from us in our communities.

## The Bible condemns violence and violent men

Many passages in the Bible speak out on the issue of violence, and GOD's attitude toward those that repeatedly use violence:

- Psalms 11:5 *The LORD trieth the righteous: but the wicked and him that loveth violence his soul hateth.*
- Zephaniah 1:9 *In the same day also will I punish all those that leap on the threshold, which fill their masters' houses with violence and deceit.*
- Psalms 37:9 *For evildoers shall be cut off: but those that wait upon the LORD, they shall inherit the earth.*
- Malachi 2:16-17 *"I hate [...] a man's covering his wife with violence, as well as with his garment." says the Lord Almighty...."You have wearied the Lord with your words." "How have we wearied him?" you ask. By saying "all who do evil are good in the eyes of the Lord, and he is pleased with them," or "Where is the God of justice?"* (NIV alternate translation)

In a similar way, 'wrath' or anger is condemned as being sinful, as is <u>sexual abuse</u>:

- James 1:19,20 *Wherefore, my beloved brethren, let every man be swift to hear, slow to speak, slow to wrath:For the wrath of man worketh not the righteousness of God.*
- Ephesians 5:3-5 *But fornication (note: that is to say, sexual immorality, including sexual abuse), and all uncleanness, or covetousness, let it not be once named among you, as becometh saints; Neither filthiness, nor foolish talking, nor jesting, which are not convenient: but rather giving of thanks. For this ye know, that no whoremonger, nor unclean person, nor covetous man, who is an idolater, hath any inheritance in the kingdom of Christ and of God*

## What the Bible says about Verbal Abuse

Scripture also shows us that the very words we speak can be considered as a form of violence:

- Proverbs 10:6 *Blessings are upon the head of the just: but violence covereth the mouth of the wicked.*
- Proverbs 10:11 *The mouth of a righteous man is a well of life: but violence covereth the mouth of the wicked.*
- Matthew 5:21,22 *Ye have heard that it was said by them of old time, Thou shalt not kill; and whosoever shall kill shall be in danger of the judgment: But I say unto you, That whosoever is angry with his brother without a cause shall be in danger of*

*the judgment: and whosoever shall say to his brother, Raca, shall be in danger of the council: but whosoever shall say, Thou fool, shall be in danger of hell fire*

As followers of Christ we are encouraged to consider everything we say to one another, whether it stands the test of being for the benefit of the hearer - verbal abuse surely does not qualify:

- Ephesians 4:29 *Let no corrupt communication proceed out of your mouth, but that which is good to the use of edifying, that it may minister grace unto the hearers.*
- James 1:26 *If any man among you seem to be religious, and bridleth not his tongue, but deceiveth his own heart, this man's religion is vain.*
- James 3:10 *Out of the same mouth proceedeth blessing and cursing. My brethren, these things ought not so to be.*
- Ephesians 4:31 *Let all bitterness, and wrath, and anger, and clamour, and evil speaking, be put away from you, with all malice:*

There is so much in Scripture as to how we are to handle the abuser but this chapter is about the abused. The Church - and each individual follower of Christ - has a responsibility to offer comfort and help to those who are oppressed (by their partner), needy (of reassurance and protection), weak (due to the constant onslaught of abuse) and in distress.

- Galatians 6:2 *Bear ye one another's burdens, and so fulfil the law of Christ.*
- Hebrews 12:12 *Wherefore lift up the hands which hang down, and the feeble knees;*
- Hebrews 13:3 *Remember them that are in bonds, as bound with them; and them which suffer adversity, as being yourselves also in the body.*
- Isaiah 1:17 *Learn to do well; seek judgment, relieve the oppressed, judge the fatherless, plead for the widow.*
- Proverbs 31:9 *Open thy mouth, judge righteously, and plead the cause of the poor and needy.*
- Jeremiah 22:3 *Thus saith the LORD; Execute ye judgment and righteousness, and deliver the spoiled out of the hand of the oppressor: and do no wrong, do no violence to the stranger, the fatherless, nor the widow, neither shed innocent blood in this place.*
- Genesis 42:21 *And they said one to another, We are verily guilty concerning our brother, in that we saw the anguish of his soul, when he besought us, and we would not hear; therefore is this distress come upon us.*
- Isaiah 35:3,4 *Strengthen ye the weak hands, and confirm the feeble knees.*
  *Say to them that are of a fearful heart, Be strong, fear not: behold, your God will come with vengeance, even God with a recompence; he will come and save you.*

It is important that you convey to them that:

## The LORD sympathizes and offers comfort to those who are afflicted

The LORD does hear our prayers, He does care when we cry. He is there to comfort, guide us and heal us.

- *Psalms 18:48 He delivereth me from mine enemies: yea, thou liftest me up above those that rise up against me: thou hast delivered me from the violent man.*
- *2 Samuel 22:28 And the afflicted people thou wilt save: but thine eyes are upon the haughty, that thou mayest bring them down.*
- *Psalms 22:24 For he hath not despised nor abhorred the affliction of the afflicted; neither hath he hid his face from him; but when he cried unto him, he heard.*
- *Psalms 140:12 I know that the LORD will maintain the cause of the afflicted, and the right of the poor.*
- *Psalms 72:14 He shall redeem their soul from deceit and violence: and precious shall their blood be in his sight.*
- *Psalms 9:9 The LORD also will be a refuge for the oppressed, a refuge in times of trouble.*
- *Psalms 103:6 The LORD executeth righteousness and judgment for all that are oppressed.*
- *Psalms 146:7 Which executeth judgment for the oppressed: which giveth food to the hungry. The LORD looseth the prisoners:*

National Domestic Violence Hotline at 1-800-799-SAFE(7233)

## <u>Child Abuse</u>

Child abuse presents a terrifying picture. Without the perspective of a loving heavenly father, it could easily lead to hopeless despair. In the Bible we read of God the creator who has made all men in his own image: 'in the image of God he created him; male and female he created them' (Gn 1:27). That in itself places an incredible value on each human life. But God's nature goes further: not only has he made man but he loves each one of us, completely and unconditionally. God's love is the fullness of all a father's love should be. Behold, what manner of love the Father hath bestowed upon us, that we should be called the sons of God: therefore the world knoweth us not, because it knew him not.' (1 Jn 3:1) God loves all men equally, yet as we read the Bible, we see a God who has a special concern for the weak and vulnerable. This includes children: But Jesus called them unto him, and said, Suffer little children to come unto me, and forbid them not: for of such is the kingdom of God.'(Lk 18:16).

When God created mankind, he instructed them to 'fill the earth and subdue it' (Gn 1:28). With this mandate, God delegated responsibilities to mankind: we all have a responsibility to love our neighbor (Lv 19:18); parents have a particular responsibility to care for and nurture their children.

So just what is Child Abuse? Child abuse is when a parent or caregiver, whether through action or failing to act, causes injury, death, emotional harm or risk of serious harm to a child. There are many forms of child maltreatment, including neglect, physical abuse, sexual abuse, exploitation, and emotional abuse, and yes unfortunately it can still be found in our communities and congregations.

- <u>Physical abuse of a child</u> is when a parent or caregiver causes any non-accidental physical injury to a child. There are many signs of physical abuse. If you see any of the following signs, please get help right away. 28.3% of adults report being physically abused as a child.
- <u>Sexual abuse</u> occurs when an adult uses a child for sexual purposes or involves a child in sexual acts. It also includes when a child who is older or more powerful uses another child for sexual gratification or excitement. 20.7% of adults report being sexually abused as a child.
- <u>Emotional abuse</u> is when a parent or caregiver harms a child's mental and social development, or causes severe emotional harm, it is considered emotional abuse. While a single incident may be abuse, most often emotional abuse is a pattern of behavior that causes damage over time. 10.6% of adults report being emotionally abused as a child.
- <u>Child neglect</u> is when a parent or caregiver does not give the care, supervision, affection and support needed for a child's health, safety and well-being. Child neglect includes:

  - ➢ Physical neglect and inadequate supervision
  - ➢ Emotional neglect
  - ➢ Medical neglect
  - ➢ Educational neglect

Once again we have a body of believers who while it is getting better, in fact, child abuse is discussed and taught so much that there is practically no secrecy in the matter and reports are being filed, there are still some who are not clear on what abuse actually is. They justify the behaviors by misquoting scripture and taking it out of context. We must never use the scripture to justify hurting or abusing a child. Because of the exposure of this form of abuse I will not spend too much time on this topic.

Matthew 18:6 states: But whoso shall offend one of these little ones which believe in me, it were better for him that a millstone were hanged about his neck, and *that* he were drowned in the depth of the sea

Child abuse denies the individual's worth. It distorts the meaning of fatherhood and it specifically targets the weak and the vulnerable. It is the epitome of Satan's work. However, we know that while Satan may be at work in this world, he is nevertheless a defeated enemy. We can still have hope: through Jesus' death on the cross, God has freely provided redemption for all men. This redemption includes healing for the abused, healing and forgiveness for the abuser and cleansing from all that has defiled us (Is 53:5; Mt 26:28; Heb 9:14). We know too that Jesus will come again - as judge and as restoring king. When he comes, Satan's power will be finally destroyed, and there will be a new heaven and a new earth with 'no more death or mourning or crying or pain' (Rev 21:4).

If you see any signs of abuse in someone you know, or if you yourself are involved in an abusive relationship, get help right away. The Childhelp National Child Abuse Hotline is a 24-hour hotline with resources to aid in every child abuse situation. All calls are anonymous and confidential **1-800-4-A-CHILD (1-800-422-4453)**

## **Elder Abuse**

Each year hundreds of thousands of older persons are abused, neglected, and exploited. Many victims are people who are older, frail, and vulnerable and cannot help themselves and depend on others to meet their most basic needs. Abusers of older adults are both women and men, and may be family members, friends, or "trusted others."

In general, elder abuse is a term referring to any knowing, intentional, or negligent act by a caregiver or any other person that causes harm or a serious risk of harm to a vulnerable adult. Legislatures in all 50 states have passed some form of elder abuse prevention laws. Laws and definitions of terms vary considerably from one state to another, but broadly defined, abuse may be:

- **Physical Abuse**—inflicting physical pain or injury on a senior, e.g. slapping, bruising, or restraining by physical or chemical means.
- **Sexual Abuse**—non-consensual sexual contact of any kind.
- **Neglect**—the failure by those responsible to provide food, shelter, health care, or protection for a vulnerable elder.
- **Exploitation**—the illegal taking, misuse, or concealment of funds, property, or assets of a senior for someone else's benefit.

- **Emotional Abuse**—inflicting mental pain, anguish, or distress on an elder person through verbal or nonverbal acts, e.g. humiliating, intimidating, or threatening.
- **Abandonment**—desertion of a vulnerable elder by anyone who has assumed the responsibility for care or custody of that person.
- **Self-neglect**—characterized as the failure of a person to perform essential, self-care tasks and that such failure threatens his/her own health or safety.

Often, the Bible does not use our terms or categories but still has much to say on the subject. The Bible has much on how older people should be treated by others. I will give you some of these teachings in no particular order.

- An older man is to be treated like a father while an older woman is to be treated like a mother. This would include treating them with respect while caring for them and their needs. 1 Timothy 5:1-2states, "Rebuke not an elder, but intreat him as a father; and the younger men as brethren; The elder women as mothers; the younger as sisters, with all purity."
- Older people are to be treated with special honor. That would include absence of physical or verbal abuse. However, it would also include listening to them with respect, honoring their desires and opinions, and giving them an exalted place. Leviticus 19:32
  says, "Thou shalt rise up before the hoary head, and honour the face of the old man, and fear thy God: I am the LORD." The "hoary head" is the head that is covered with grey hairs. To rise up before them means to stand and show them honor when they enter the room. I understand that this is the law, but there are many lessons for us here. In the book of Job, Elihu waited to speak until all the older men had their say (Job 32:4).
- As one of the signs of a society that has broken down and rejected God, "the child shall behave himself proudly against the ancient" (Isaiah 3:5). It is wrong to mistreat the elderly.
- We are warned against the mistreatment of our parents when they grow old. Proverbs 23:22
  states, "Hearken unto thy father that begat thee, and despise not thy mother when she is old." Jesus is our example in this because He made sure that His mother had someone to care for her even as He suffered on the cross (see John 19:26-27). Even nephews are responsible for widowed aunts if there are no children (1 Timothy 5:4).
- The Bible even goes so far as requiring us to follow the lead of the elder. In Philemon 1:9
  , Paul pleaded as "Paul the aged." It was assumed that his age brought increased respect for what he had to say. 1 Peter 5:5
  teaches, "Likewise, ye younger, submit yourselves unto the elder." This really goes

against our thinking today when we have accepted youth as one of our gods. Yet it is the teaching of the Bible. Certainly, there are times when older people would lead us away from the commands of God and this advice cannot be righteously followed. However, the Bible is clear. We are to give in to them whenever possible and follow their wisdom and leadership when it does not go against the clear teaching of God's word.

I understand that most of these verse do not deal directly with the kinds of elder abuse we often hear about in the news today. However, it does not need to. If these principles are followed; if we honor our elders, give them special place, and submit to them, we can never physically or verbally abuse them. I hope this helps.

## **Religious Abuse**

The dictionary simply defines Religious abuse as "to abuse administered under the guise of religion, including harassment or humiliation, possibly resulting in psychological trauma. Religious abuse may also include misuse of religion for selfish, secular, or ideological ends such as the abuse of a clerical position. This however does not really give us a clear picture of what "Religious Abuse" is.

What is "religious abuse?" Religious abuse is the mistreatment of a person by someone in spiritual authority, resulting in a diminishing of that person's sense of growth and well-being both spiritually and emotionally. This spiritual authority is used to manipulate others for personal gain to achieve a personal agenda, thereby harming that person's walk with God. It can further be defined as any misuse of Scripture that harms a person's relationship with God. Lastly it is the damage resulting from cult involvement.

Spiritual Abuse is one of the clearest and most precisely defined teachings to be found in the pages of the Bible, even though it is not presented under that name. When one considers the fact that it is a significant theme in the Old Testament prophets, that our Lord Jesus Christ devoted a considerable portion of His ministry to addressing it, and that every single New Testament author mentions it in some form or in some way, we might sooner question our own Christianity -- or at least our knowledge of Scripture -- than question the objective definability of Spiritual Abuse.

The writings of the Old Testament prophets are filled with examples and denunciations of Spiritual Abuse, but perhaps the clearest words ever uttered by such a prophet on the subject of spiritual abuse are found in Ezekiel chapter 34, where we read:

And the word of the LORD came unto me, saying, Son of man, prophesy against the shepherds of Israel, prophesy, and say unto them, Thus saith the Lord GOD unto the shepherds; Woe be to the shepherds of Israel that do feed themselves! should not the shepherds feed the flocks? Ye eat the fat, and ye clothe you with the wool, ye kill them that are fed: but ye feed not the flock. The diseased have ye not strengthened, neither have ye healed that which was sick, neither have ye bound up that which was broken, neither have ye brought again that which was driven away, neither have ye sought that which was lost; but with force and with cruelty have ye ruled them. And they were scattered, because there is no shepherd: and they became meat to all the beasts of the field, when they were scattered. My sheep wandered through all the mountains, and upon every high hill: yea, my flock was scattered upon all the face of the earth, and none did search or seek after them. (1-6)

"Spiritual Abuse" does exist, according to the Bible, and in this brief passage we can see some of the characteristics that the current Spiritual Abuse literature ascribes to it. Ezekiel was identifying a form of mistreatment which was spiritual in nature, because it mistreated people by hindering their relationship with God. It was (and is) characterized by oppression and neglect.

For the most part, spiritual abuse is committed by those who sincerely love Jesus, who believe the Bible to be the Word of God and who want to win lost souls for Jesus. Hence, spiritual abuse can often be found, as Ronald Enroth points out, in churches that are doctrinally sound, conservatively Christian, thoroughly Biblical, and zealously maintaining the fundamentals of the Faith. There are several reasons why Christian people of good will and a sincere desire to share Jesus can inflict serious harm and injury upon others in the Name of Jesus. Lack of Empathy. Empathy is the ability to perceive, to understand, to sense, to feel what another person is experiencing. Unfortunately, in witnessing for Jesus many evangelicals talk to people, not with people. It is impossible to truly talk with anyone about Jesus, or anything else for that matter, without knowing the other person. Authentic ministry is based upon knowing a person. There is no point in claiming that Jesus is the answer, when you have not heard the question. A physician who prescribes medicine without knowing the patient is likely to injure the patient. In like manner, evangelicals who try to minister without knowing the sheep in an empathic manner will most likely injure it.

Due to the breadth of this topic I am not going into it at this time because religious abuse spans from being in a legalistic church, through, worshiping under a narcissistic leader to being indoctrinated into a cult. What is important is that we understand that this may be the condition of someone sitting in the pew or on the porch with us. Understanding this is the first step to seeing why they are the way that they are and why they respond to things of the church the way that they do. In workshops I will go deeper into this as well as handle questions but for now we will leave it at this.

The following are very good books that will help you are those whom you love recover from this form of abuse:

> ➤ **Recovering from Religious Abuse: 11 Steps to Spiritual Freedom**
>     By Jack Watts, Robert S. McGee

> ➤ **Toxic Faith: Experiencing Healing Over Painful Spiritual Abuse**
>                                                                                     By
>
>     Stephen Arterburn, Jack Felton

So now that we have reviewed the various forms of abuse you may be asking yourself, what is it that I can do to help?

Here are five things that you can do if you know someone who is in an abusive relationship.

1. ***Listen hard, speak little***. People who disclose problems at home usually feel a great deal of shame. It's already difficult for them to talk about it, but when we jump in with our response or offer a solution, we often shut them down or give unwise or trite answers to a very painful and complex problem. Proverbs says, "He who answers before he hears, it is his folly and shame" (Proverbs 18:13).

2. ***Validate their experience***. It's normal to feel afraid to tell a family secret. It's common to blame oneself for one's partner's abusive behaviors. Don't minimize, trivialize, or rationalize things away. Saying things like, "I can't believe what you're saying, or he or she seems so nice or godly or normal" is hurtful.

Instead say things like, "It was good that you told someone." Or "I can't imagine what you're going through, but telling is the first step to getting help." Or "No matter how you disappoint your husband (or wife), you don't deserve to be treated this way."

3. ***Pray***. We often forget how potent prayer is. Even when we don't know the whole story, God does. Sometimes we feel helpless to really know what to do in these kinds of situations. Prayer is an important reminder that God is in charge and loves both the abused and the abuser. We must bring the situation before God daily, asking Him to intervene in a way that we cannot imagine.

4. ***Offer tangible help***. James says, "Suppose you see a brother or sister who needs food or clothing and you say, 'Well, good-bye and God bless you; stay warm and eat well' – but then

you don't give that person any food or clothing. What good does that do? So you see, it isn't enough just to have faith. Faith that doesn't show itself by good deeds is no faith at all – it is dead and useless." (James 2:16,17).

Does the person need medical attention? Counseling help? Legal aid? A safe place to live? Sometimes people need concrete support to break free from abusive patterns and it takes the loving and tangible resources of a community of people to help them. The Good Samaritan didn't just pray, he also carted the broken and battered person to the inn and paid for his care.

**_5. Advocate and/or report where needed and appropriate._** If you are a mandated reporter and a child discloses that he/she has been a victim of abuse, you must report this disclosure to the proper authorities. However an adult victim of spousal abuse needs an advocate too. Someone who will come along side of him/her and speak with community agencies, attend legal proceedings and help communicate with church leaders in order to have the best possible hope for repentance, healing, and reconciliation of the family.

Regardless to the type of abuse the person that you are helping is a victim of, it is important that you help them to remember that in Christ you are never alone. As Matthew 5:3-10 records:

**"Blessed are the poor in spirit, for theirs is the kingdom of heaven. Blessed are those who mourn, for they will be comforted. Blessed are the meek, for they will inherit the earth. Blessed are those who hunger and thirst for righteousness, for they will be filled. Blessed are the merciful, for they will be shown mercy. Blessed are the pure in heart, for they will see God. Blessed are the peacemakers, for they will be called sons of God. Blessed are those who are persecuted because of righteousness, for theirs is the kingdom of heaven".**

We may not be able to do everything needed to stem the tide of violence at home, but we certainly can do something. What can you do today?

*LOVE YOUR MEMBER TO LIFE!!!!!*

# ~ After Care ~

Wow, you have just completed your first assignment. You stopped, noticed, had compassion, used all of your learning and actually helped someone. You are exhausted aren't you? Little did you know that it would be so hard, require so much of yourself, and last longer than one sit down conversation? You have heard stories that have broken your heart, pushed the limits of you peace and patience. You have had to make some hard decisions. Some decisions that were in the best interest of the person you were helping, as in the case of abuse and addictions. Some decisions that alienated you from fellow parishioners or neighbors as in keeping confidence and loving the unlovable while advocating for them. You have carried a burden you did not create and walked into and out of a storm that was not yours. But Praise God with His help and your willingness and availability you did it. And now you are exhausted and you are heavy. After all carrying yourself is difficult enough but now you have the weight of someone else added to you. What do you do?

After care is so very important. Just like you need to prepare for your mission encounter, you need to debrief from it. The first thing that I learned as I was prepping for my profession was that all good psychologists have their own psychologist. I remember thinking, I'm strong enough to handle it. I can leave it in the office and if not I'll just stop by the church on my way home and give it all to the Lord. I was so wrong on many counts. I could not leave it in the office. These are real people not pages in a book, you get touched by their experience. After all Paul tells us in Romans the 12th chapter to Love without dissimulation, be kindly affectioned one to another with brotherly love; in honour preferring one another, rejoicing in hope; patient in tribulation; continuing instant in prayer; distributing to the necessity of saints rejoicing with them that do rejoice, and weeping with them that weep, not being overcome of evil, but overcoming evil with good. You have cried out to the Lord in intercession for this person and He has used you in answer to prayer. You will need someplace to dispose of all of this that has attached itself to you in the process.

Confidentiality is the principle thing. People have trusted you so if you must share you cannot share in a way that will cause their identity to be discovered. It is preferred not to share in the same church or community. But share you must. And there are a few ways in which you can share.

1. The first way is through a tool that you have used in the accompanying workbook to this book. It is called "journaling" This is a safe place for you to put it all down and get it all out. The best type of journals in this technological age that we live in today is your computer in a password protected file. This keeps it from being able to be picked up and "accidently

read" or "discussed in the open" It keeps the person safe as well as your thought, feelings and working through as you walked through this journey with this person.

2. Another is a full well. Every person need at least one full well in their life. You have just been a full well to someone. It is my suggestion that if you have three full wells you will be most successful. A full well is someone with whom you can be you. You can say what you feel without worry or recrimination or breach of confidentiality. A full well is one who will tell you the truth no matter how hard it is or how unpleasant it is to hear. They know how to "LISTEN" and not speak and they know the appropriate time to speak. Make sure that you have a full well that is nowhere near the people and or situations with which you have just helped who can speak life back into you and build you back up.

3. There is nothing like a hobby. Sadly in the church world today, many are caught up in so many programs and mandatory settings that there is no time to just relax. Look at the word recreation for a minute. Now let's dissect it. RE CREATION. That is what down town or hobby's do. They help to recreate you to your optimal level of functioning. It relaxed you and helps in the cell regeneration process. If you like to read, always have a book available that you can sit down and lose yourself in for a few hours to a couple of days. If you play an instrument, play until this person is lifted off of you. This is actually a biblical principal. As David prayed the spirit within Saul calmed down.

4. This one might be challenging if you are a shower person, but soaking in a tub for a minimum of 20 minutes with dim lights and soft music will work wonders.

5. Exercise is wonderful. It will get those endorphins firing and naturally help you to feel better.

6. Last but not least, lose yourself in praise. Praise just makes a body feel good.

You may have some methods of your own if you are the type of person who takes good emotional care of yourself. The important thing is that you do something to restore yourself as you finish your assignment. Scripture is full of examples of this type of after care. Take the time to search the scriptures and give yourself permission to take care of you.

# ~ EPILOGUE ~

## ~ MILITARY MATTERS ~

## ~ *MILITARY MATTERS* ~

### *FROM MY HEART TO YOURS*

I really in my heart of hearts wanted to deal with the special population of the military and their families. The research was so overwhelming and the personal accounts that I received from both combat service members and combat veterans along with those serving who have not been deployed yet face challenges and mindsets in their churches and communities as well as family members from all of the above flooded me. I could not get it all down in one chapter and do it justice.

I want to take this time to formally apologize to all of those who have served and are serving in our armed forces. I also want to apologize to their spouses and children. I give you my word that at ever training that I facilitate for certification in Called to Care you will be included. There will be a dialogue concerning you. I give you my word that your life and your sacrifice will not be generalized, trivialized nor victimized in any way. I give my word to you that I will do my best to write an accompanying manual of Called to Care that deals specifically with your population.

To you, the readers. As of the time of this writing our country has been at war for 14 years. We have so many wounded warriors and silent sufferers that it is hard to wrap one's mind around it. Perhaps we continue as if this is not happening because this war is not being fought on our soil. Perhaps it is because the residue has not come home to sit on our front porches that we have lost the ability to be touched by what is happening. But it is a reality that we need to have a discussion about. The truth is that until we do this population will suffer in silence in our communities and churches.

One thing that I would like to share here is that in the 239 years that America has been a country it has been at war 222 years. That is 93% of our existence. Somewhere along the span of time we have forgotten the tremendous sacrifice that has been made. They go to defend us. They come home some in bags, some with noticeable changes such as loss of limbs, sight, and cognition. Some with emotional scars that are easily seen like PTSD and TBI. But may come home with wounds that you cannot see such as survivor's guilt, or being unable to forgive themselves for what they have seen and participated in. Many feel unworthy of life upon return and we with our lack of compassion do not help.

Many of our returning soldiers are forced out of the military because they are no longer deployable. They are left to a thankless community, unemployed, on a ridiculously long waiting list for evaluation for benefits from the VA, feeling a loss of a life cut short due to injury. Many are greeted not with our thanks or gratitude but with distain or normalcy as if what they have sacrificed doesn't even matter. Marriages are destroyed because we teach our soldiers how to leave but we do not teach them how to come home. Spouses are ill equipped to handle the changes and challenges that come into their homes. Children remember one parent and the new normal is nothing like what left. Yet in our churches they are expected to not miss a beat. After all most churches have a population of veterans who talk about the "glory days" yet are so far removed perhaps they fail to remember what life was really like. Is it that the souses have forgotten what it was like to hold their breath waiting on that moral call or letter to make its way through? Have the children now grown forgotten about the nightmares that "daddy or mommy has died in the war" or days trying to understand why "Daddy is going to kill someone who didn't do anything to them" or struggling with the concept of war when the bible says not to kill? Have we forgotten the sigh of relief when our loved one made it off of that plane, train or boat and held us in their arms and we were so glad that they were home…or the tears of confusion and pain of reunification as you realized that all of you had changed because of this separation…the fear that we will never recover what we as a couple, a family lost? Did you forget going to church for help and healing to be met with questions as to why you missed this service or that service or this donation or that or be thrust into activities that pulled you away from what mattered the most…the ministry of reconciliation and restoration?

Maybe you have never served nor had a loved on serve so you do not understand. Maybe you never deployed nor had a loved one to deploy, but it is my prayer that this little tidbit will help you to see what there is a need for a book such as this and the training to help compassionately care about this population. It is also my prayer that you will see why to deal with this population properly, I felt the need to exclude it from this book but feel the unction to provide a separate platform for it.

Again, thank you to all you submitted material and anecdotal information in the preparation of this chapter. You opened my heart and my soul wider that it was before. I thought that I had and understanding before with all of the military members in my family growing up spanning several wars, from being a retired military spouse, being the mother of a combat veteran (my only daughter) and from all of the military students that I encounter term after term after term. I was so wrong. When I asked, the flood gates opened and I was moved with compassion. Thank you for educating, the educator.

## ~ CLOSING COMMENT ~

Thank you so much for spending this time with me as we discuss the Special Populations that are in your congregations and communities. Thank you so much for taking the time to actually *see* the needs. Thank you for not just looking on the situations but allowing yourself to be the instrument that the Lord can use to actually *help*. This could only have been achieved by allowing yourself not to be hardened by life's experiences or buying into the mindset of a world who is quickly forgetting all that Jesus not only came here to do, but commissioned us as believers to do also. Jesus said in John 14:*12 "Verily, verily, I say unto you, He that believeth on me, the works that I do shall he do also; and greater works than these shall he do; because I go unto my Father."* I want to thank you for being moved with compassion and caring about these members of special populations enough to put feet to you prayers and be *moved* with compassion. Finally I would like to thank you for understanding that whether or not you have a credential, position, influence, fame, or a religious institution that you belong to you have been first and foremost Called to Care!

May the Lord richly bless you, keep you, sustain you and comfort you along your journey.

# References

Kubler-Ross, E. (1969). *On death and dying.* New York: Macmillan.

http://www.merriam-webster.com/dictionary/citation.

Levy, A. (2000).*The Orphaned Adult* Da Capo Press.

http://www.nakeddivorce.com/blog/divorce-grieving-cycle/

http://www.divorceessentials.net/tag/hard-choices/

http://www.indyweek.com/indyweek/a-support-group-straight-talk-helps-families-of-prisoners/Content?oid=3633903

http://thomrainer.com/2014/01/08/seven-things-we-learned-from-pastors-kids/

http://ryanhuguley.com/ryan-huguley/2013/12/16/5-ways-to-love-your-pastors-kids

http://www.bandbacktogether.com

http://www.iwilltrustinyou.org

http://kidshealth.org/kid/feeling/friend/special_needs.html

http://www.parentcenterhub.org/repository/notalone/

http://www.nopointsforstyle.com/2013/08/dear-people-who-do-not-have-a-child-with-disabilities.html

American Psychiatric Association. (2013). *Diagnostic and statistical manual of mental disorders* (5th ed.). Washington, DC: Author.

http://www.trueorigin.org/gaygene01.php

https://www.genome.gov/DNADay/q.cfm?aid=347&year=2012

http://www.goldencradle.org/how-do-children-same-sex-adoption-fare

http://www.asam.org/for-the-public/definition-of-addiction

DR. PATRICIA LOTT

# ABOUT THE AUTHOR

Dr. Patricia Lott gave her life to the Lord at age 16 and has been striving daily to take the words of the Lord from the Page to the Life. She believes that it is not enough to have faith to be saved but that we must have an active faith that calls us to action. She strives daily to touch humanity in the way the Lord has touched her.

Shacklebuster Ministries is a work that the Lord birthed in her after calling her to look and see the condition of His house and His people. She was moved to action seeing the shackles and burdens that we walk around with and said "Yes Lord, you can use me to aid in the deliverance of your people." The Shacklebuster Conference is an anointed experience that you will never forget!

Remaining faithful to the Lord Dr. Lott said "yes" when the Lord called her again to add "Called to Care" workshops to the ministry.

Dr. Lott is the First Lady of Cornerstone Community COGIC, a marriage and family therapist, college professor and author of the Marcie Mouse book Series, the Little Cherub book series and Shacklebusting Scripture Studies. She is also a much requested revivalist, conference speaker and workshop facilitator. Her ministry remains to heal the broken hearted and to challenge others to live a life reflective of the relationship they say they have with Christ. With all of this to her charge you will be hard pressed to find a more down to earth lover of all people than she.

www.ingramcontent.com/pod-product-compliance
Lightning Source LLC
LaVergne TN
LVHW061225060426
835509LV00012B/1425